POEMS FOR THE HAZARA
A MULTILINGUAL POETRY ANTHOLOGY
AND COLLABORATIVE POEM

English, Spanish, Catalan, Japanese, Norwegian, Turkey,
Hazaragi, Italian, Greek, German, Irish, Hebrew,
Romanian, French, Armenian, Hungarian and Portuguese

POEMS FOR THE HAZARA

A MULTILINGUAL POETRY ANTHOLOGY AND COLLABORATIVE POEM

BY 125 POETS FROM 68 COUNTRIES

Executive Editor

Kamran Mir Hazar

FULL PAGE PUBLISHING

2014

POEMS FOR THE HAZARA
A MULTILINGUAL POETRY ANTHOLOGY AND
COLLABORATIVE POEM
Executive Editor Kamran Mir Hazar

ISBN: 978-0-9837708-2-4 (hardcover)
ISBN: 978-0-9837708-6-2 (paperback)
ISBN: 978-0-9837708-7-9 (e-book)

First Edition: February 2014
Library of Congress Control Number: 2013958327

Copyright © 2014 by Kamran Mir Hazar

All rights reserved. To re-publish a poem(s) by a single poet in this book, you need prior written permission of the poet.
www.HazaraRights.com

Cover: Photograph of Buddha in Bamiyan, courtesy of Najibullah Mosafer. Flag of Hazaristan, yellow, white and blue, designed by Kamran Mir Hazar may be used freely.

Without limiting the rights copyright reserved above, no part of this publication may be reproduced, stored in or introduced into a retrieval system, or transmitted, in any form or by any means (electronic, mechanical, photocopying, recording or otherwise).

Full Page Publishing
411 Walnut Street
Davidson, NC 28036 USA
www.FullPagePublishing.com

DEDICATED TO THE HAZARA

Contents

Acknowledgments	i
Etnairis Ribera, Puerto Rico	3
My Name Is Fatima Of Hazaristan	5
Me Llamo Fátima De Hazaristán (Spanish)	7
Angelina Llongueras, Catalonia	9
A Poem In Catalan For The Hazara People	11
Poema En Català Pel Poble Hazara (Catalan)	16
Aju Mukhopadhyay, Pondicherry, India	21
In Reasonable Support Of The Hazara People	23
The Victims Of The Evil Forces	25
Ban'ya Natsuishi, Japan	27
Haiku For Hazara People (English And Japanese)	29
Julio Pavanetti, Uruguay/Spain	34
The Voice Of All Of Us	36
La Voz De Todos (Spanish)	38
Gertrude Fester, Rwanda/ South Africa	40
Hope For The Hazaras	42
Homage To The Hazara People	43
Jack Hirschman, USA	45
Six Haikus	46
Iztok Osojnik, Slovenia	52
For The Hazara People	54
Erling Kittelsen, Norway	58
Human- Hazara	60
Menneske-Hazara (Norwegian)	61

Obediah Michael Smith, Bahamas   62
Hazaristan   64
Hazaristan Among Rugged Mountains   67

Bina Sarkar Ellias, India   72
Untitled Poem   73

Raúl Henao, Colombia   76
Hazara   78
Hazara (Spanish)   79

Anne Waldman, USA   80
Speak For The Hazara   81

Nguyen Quang Thieu, Vietnam   82
Last Night A Hazara Baby Was Born   84

Timo Berger, Germany   86
In The East   87
En El Este (Spanish)   90

Elsa Tió, Puerto Rico   93
Hazara   94
Hazara (Spanish)   96

Kamran Mir Hazar, Hazaristan   98
With Haiku's Body/ 30 Poems (English, Hazaragi And Italian)   99

Rodrigo Verdugo, Chile   129
Hazara, We Will Speak Your Language   131
Hazara Hablaremos Tu Lengua (Spanish)   132

Mildred Kiconco Barya, Uganda   133
Here And Now: Hazara   134

Stefaan Van Den Bremt, Flanders, Belgium   135
Untitled Poem   136
Untitled Poem (Spanish)   137

Winston Morales Chavarro, Colombia — 138
Hazara — 140
Hazara (Spanish) — 142

Esteban Valdés Arzate, Mexico — 144
Star Sonnet — 145

Akwasi Aidoo, Ghana/USA — 146
This-Crime-Nation — 147

Yolanda Pantin, Venezuela — 148
Bamiyan — 150
Bamiyán (Spanish) — 151

Yiorgos Chouliaras, Greece — 152
Hazara — 154
Refugees — 155
Πρoσφυγεσ (Greek) — 156

James O'hara, Mexico/Usa/Ireland — 157
Crash The Sun — 158

Raquel Chalfi, Israel — 159
Precipice — 160

Jim Byron, USA — 162
Liberty, Come Galloping! Salvation, Flower! — 163

Luisa Vicioso Sánchez, Dominican Republic — 165
Haiti (Hazara) — 166
Haiti (Hazara) (Spanish) — 168

Andrea Garbin, Italy — 170
Untitled Poem — 172
Untitled Poem (Italian) — 173

Luz Helena Cordero Villamizar, Colombia — 174
Verses Like Paths — 176
Versos Como Caminos (Spanish) — 177

Peter Voelker, Germany	178
New Sights	180
On Art And Love	181
Über Die Kunst Und Die Liebe (German)	182
Neuer Blick (German)	183
Zoran Anchevski, Macedonia	184
Emigrants' Poem	186
Naotaka Uematsu, Japan	188
War And Children (English And Japanese)	189
Tanka Dedicated To The Hazara (English And Japanese)	190
Paul Disnard, Colombia	191
Hazara	192
Hazara (Spanish)	194
Vyacheslav Kupriyanov, Russia	196
Appel	197
Llamamiento (Spanish)	198
Gabriel Rosenstock, Ireland	199
Squid: Photo Of An Embryo	201
Máthair Shúigh: Grianghraf De Ghin (Irish)	202
Maruja Vieira, Colombia	204
Hazara	206
Hazara (Spanish)	207
Nyein Way, Myanmar	208
Peace	209
Gaston Bellemare, Québec	210
Untitled Poem	212
Untitled Poem (French)	213
Zohra Hamid, South Africa	214
Why	215
Land Or Air	217

Amir Or, Israel	218
The Barbarians (Round Two)	220
הַבַּרְבָּרִים: סִבּוּב שֵׁנִי (Hebrew)	221
Ivan Djeparoski, Macedonia	222
Unheimlich	223
Attila F. Balázs, Slovakia	224
Statuesque Stubbornness	226
History	227
Ioana Trica, Romania	228
The Cherry Tree's Time Of Fire	230
Ora De Foc A Cireşului (Romanian)	231
Michaël Glück, France	232
Untitled Poem	233
Quito Nicolaas, The Netherlands	235
Betrayal	237
Conversations	239
Noria Adel, Algeria	241
Untitled Poem	242
Untitled Poem (French)	243
Francisco Sánchez Jiménez, Colombia	244
Hazara In My Thoughts	245
Hazara En Mi Pensamiento (Spanish)	247
Werewere Liking, Cameroon/ Ivory Coast	249
"I Am Love" Say The Voices In The Bellies Of Women	251
Ou «Suis L'amour» Disent Les Voix De Ventres De Femmes... (French)	254
Beppe Costa, Italy	258
Heroin/Heroine	259
William Pérez Vega, Puerto Rico	260
I Have Only Words	262

Solo Tengo Palabras (Spanish)   264

Angelee Deodhar, India   266
The Road To Bamyan   267

Fanny Moreno, Colombia   268
Silent War   270

John Curl, USA   271
How Long Hazara   272

Kevin Kiely, Ireland   273
We Are Winos!   275

Azam Abidov, Uzbekistan   277
A Poem Of Equality   279

Luis Galar (No Country)   282
Radio   283
Radio (Spanish)   284

Santiago B. Villafania, Philippines   285
Sonnet To A Pilgrim Soul   287

Althea Romeo-Mark, Antigua   288
The Forsaken   290

Bengt Berg, Sweden   291
To My Hazara Friends   292

Luz Lescure, Panama   293
Femicide   294
Femicidio (Spanish)   295

Lola Koundakjian, Armenia   296
Life   298
Կեանք (Armenian)   299

Zindzi Mandela, South Africa   300
Untitled Poem   301

Edvino Ugolini, Italy   302
You Are Not Alone   303
Non Siete Soli (Italian)   304

Jean-Claude Awono, Cameroon   305
The News Is Good   306
Les Nouvelles Sont Bonnes (French)   307

Stefania Battistella, Italy   308
Humans   309

Eugenia Sánchez Nieto, Colombia   310
Scars   312
Cicatrices (Spanish)   314

Alina Beatrice Chesca, Romania   316
The Poetry Of Hazara   218
Letter To God   320

Simón Zavala Guzmán, Ecuador   322
Freedom Flower   323
Flor De Libertad (Spanish)   325

Ostap Nozhak, Ukraine   327
Hazara   329
Хазара (Ukrainian)   330

Berry Heart, Botswana   331
A Poem For Hazara People   333

Gilma De Los Ríos, Colombia   334
The Vigil   336
La Vigilia (Spanish)   337

Laura Hernandez Muñoz, México   338
Far From Heaven   339

Mamang Dai, India   340
Untitled Poem   342

Erkut Tokman, Turkey   343
I Remember What Means Hazara   345
Hatirliyorum Hazara Ne Anlama Gelir (Turkish)   346

Álvaro Miranda, Colombia   347
A Moon For The Hazaras   348
Una Luna Para Los Hazaras (Spanish)   349

Claus Ankersen, Denmark   350
Voice Of The Voiceless   352

Mark Lipman, USA   355
Thousand   357
Who's Your Hero?   360

John Hegley, England   361
I Observe The List Of Hazara Proverbs   362

Micere Githae Mugo, Kenya   363
Hazara People And History Live On!   365

Germain Droogenbroodt, Belgium/Spain   366
Fuge Of Death (Anno 2013)   367
Peaceful Morning In The Himalayas   368

Fiyinfoluwa Onarinde, Nigeria   369
Long Before The Gathering Twilight…   371

Ataol Behramoğlu, Turkey   373
Babies Don't Have Nations   375
Bebeklerin Ulusu Yok (Turkish)   377

Khal Torabully, Mauritius/France   379
Soul Of Hazaras   380

Jorge Boccanera, Argentina   381
Nazim Hikmet's Eyes Speak   382

Hablan Los Ojos De Nazim Hikmet (Spanish) 383

Kamanda Kama Sywor, Congo 384
Atonement 386
The Blood Of Silences 387
Bitterness 388
Intimate Excerpt 389
From The Beyond 390
Prophecy 391

Bineesh Puthuppanam, India 392
Within... 393

Iris Miranda, Puerto Rico 394
The Power Of A Poem 396

Pamela Ateka, Kenya 397
Untitled Poem 398

Fahredin Shehu, Kosovo 399
O Human 400

Tamer Öncul, Cyprus 401
Smokey Earth 403
Our Wall 404
Dumanli Toprak 406
Duvarimiz 407

Tânia Tomé, Mozambique 409
Mupipi (My Bird) 491
Mupipi (My Bird) (Portuguese) 492

Howard A. Fergus, Montserrat, West Indies 412
Solidarity 413

Janak Sapkota, Nepal 414
A Haiku 415

Károly Fellinger, Hungary 416
Flower Song 418

Virágének (Hungarian)   419

Alfred Tembo, Zambia   420
Tears Of Memory   421

Emilce Strucchi, Argentina   422
Do Not   423
No (Spanish)   425

Juan Diego Tamayo, Colombia   427
Untitled Poem   428
Untitled Poem (Spanish)   429

Manuel Silva Acevedo, Chile   430
Wolves And Sheep   431

Elias Letelier, Chile   442
I Saw   444

Mohammed Bennis, Morocco   445
View   446

Károly Sándor Pallai, Hungary   447
Dalil'dera   449

Edgardo Nieves-Mieles, Puerto Rico   451
Bachata Para Un Ahogado Sin Papeles (Spanish)   453

Fatoumata Ba, Mali   464
Meditation   465

Vupenyu Otis Zvoushe, Zimbabwe   467
My Dear Hazara   468

Santosh Alex, India   469
Afghanistan   471

Silvana Berki, Albania/ Finland   473
I Guess,   475
Remember!   476

Like A Butterfly!	477
What Matter Is Justice!	478
Out Of The System	480
Sinner!	482

Hussein Habasch, Kurdistan/ Syria — 483
Umbrella	485
Forgetfulness	486
Two Trees	487
The Love Of Two Trees	488
A Tree's Dream	489

Lucy Cristina Chau, Panamá — 490
I Wish	491

A Collaborative Poem For The Hazara People (Biographies) — 493

Jessie Kleemann, Greenland — 495

Siki Dlanga, South Africa — 497

Irena Matijašević, Croatia — 498

Boel Schenlaer, Sweden — 500

Merlie M. Alunan, Philippines — 502

Ernesto P. Santiago, Philippines — 503

Rassool Snyman, South Africa — 504

Mary Smith, Scotland — 505

K. Satchidanandan, India — 507

Sukrita Paul Kumar, India — 509

Birgitta Jónsdóttir, Iceland — 511

Zelma White, Montserrat/ BWI	513
Navkirat Sodhi, India	515
Gémino H. Abad, Philippines	517
Mbizo Chirasha, Zimbabwe	519
Joyce Ashuntantang, Cameroon/USA	520

A Collaborative Poem For The Hazara — 522

An Open Letter From World-Wide Poets Addressed To World Political Leaders — 542

Translators	566
Photo Credits	567

ACKNOWLEDGMENTS

I would like to thank all poets who contributed to this anthology and collaborative poem. I would also like to thank all the translators, proof-readers, and photographers, as well as the poets, writers and activists who have signed our open letter in solidarity to the Hazara.

Special thanks to my friends, Robert Maier, Jack Hirschman, Iris Miranda, Fernando Rendón, Ban'ya Natsuishi, Birgitta Jónsdóttir and Zahra Mir Hazar.

Etnairis Ribera
Puerto Rico

Etnairis Ribera was born and lives by the sea in San Juan, Puerto Rico. A member of the Puerto Rican Poetic Generation of the 70's, she is one of the most distinguished contemporary writers of her country. Her poetry has won awards, including the *Great Award of Literature for Lifetime Excellence* given by the P.E.N. Club of Puerto Rico in 2008. Her work has been translated into English, Italian, French, Portuguese, Swedish, and Arabic and has been published in bilingual books, international anthologies, and reviews.

Etnairis participates in International Book Fairs and International Poetry Festivals: Medellín, Colombia; Granada, Nicaragua, La Habana, Cuba; Dominican Republic; San José, Costa Rica; Quetzaltenango, Guatemala, among others. Guest writer at Pablo Neruda's Museum House at Valparaíso, Chile, on the Poet's Centennial Celebration, 2004, she has presented her poetry in cities across Latin America, Spain, Portugal, Italy, and the United States. Etnairis Ribera is a Full Professor of Hispanic Literature at the University of Puerto Rico, a Translator into English and a Yoga and

Meditation Instructor. Spanish is her native language and she knows other four languages. Her great interest in the World's Natural Beauty, Art and History, makes her a traveler through the West and the East.

Etnairis has published fourteen books, among them: *A(MAR)ES, Ariadne of the Water, The Birds of the Goddess, Return to the Sea, Memories of a Poem and its Apple, The Journey of Kisses, Among Cities and Almost Paradises, The Day of the Pollen, Song of Mother Earth.*

MY NAME IS FATIMA OF HAZARISTAN

My name is Fatima of Hazaristan. Today, I am twelve years old, but there wasn't any celebration.
I'm wearing the same multicolor dress as always and my cracked skin of cold scarcity.
My grandmother used to tell me that her grandmother rode in a she-mule through the perilous path where life falls.
My colors go from the dream to the pain. Surviving, I carry on my back our arid millennial history.

In June, my heart revives like the lake in springtime. My delight is bathing in the cold waters of the Lazir River
in Nili, Daikundi. I still play with my arch under the sky of the High Valley of Kisson and I throw my small stones
towards hope, to some place where I can rest. In my mud hut, I don't understand the fear that hunts us
nor the tiny window to the world, like prison bars.

The mountains of pure violet rocks without any leaves in Panjoo surround me, while I weave my white veil
like the white almond trees that remind me the secrets of our origin.
At sunset, like a prism, the mountains draw our faces in the course of time
and awake on my forehead the huge blue eye of Band-e Amir's Lake.

My mother and my sisters weave the carpets in the fall. I learn with them to raise my sight like a mountain
that crosses the clouds in Waras. The red clouds are painted with my blood spilled in my hidden treasure.
And I contemplate them in my poor dress of all colors, with the water and the bread of my ancestors
under the snow…They call me that one without a quiet place to rightfully live, but I am Fatima of Hazaristan.

I fear death not only arrives with the hard snowfall of Dai Kundi but with the men of bad fire eyes that don't know
about compassion. I fly with the Big Crane among the rare species of birds, but the men with the bad fire
in their eyes don't let me emigrate to joyfulness. I listen to my great grandmother's song through the perilous path
and keep on hoping that the everlasting peace of Bayman's Buddha may flourish.

Translation: Etnairis Ribera

ME LLAMO FÁTIMA DE HAZARISTÁN

Me llamo Fátima de Hazaristán. Hoy cumplí doce años, pero no hubo celebración.

Llevo el mismo vestido multicolor de siempre y mi piel cuarteada por la fría escasez.

Mi abuela me contaba que su abuela cabalgó en mula por el peligroso sendero donde la vida se despeña.

Mis colores van del sueño a la pena. Sobrevivo y en mi espalda cargo nuestra árida historia milenaria.

En junio, mi corazón revive como el lago de la primavera. Mi delicia es bañarme en las aguas frías del Río Lazir
en Nili, Daikundi. Aún juego con mi arco en el ciclo del Alto Valle de Kissonn y lanzo mis pequeñas piedras
a la esperanza, hacia algún lugar donde pueda descansar. Desde mi choza de barro, no entiendo el miedo
que nos persigue ni la diminuta ventana al mundo, como rejilla carcelaria.

Las montanas de pura roca violácea sin hoja alguna en Panjaoo me rodean mientras tejo mi velo blanco
como los árboles blanquecinos del almendro que me cuentan los secretos de nuestro origen.

Al atardecer, como un prisma, las montañas dibujan nuestros rostros en el tiempo
y despiertan en mi frente el inmenso ojo azul del Lago en Band-e Amir.

Mi madre y mis hermanas tejen alfombras en el otoño. Aprendo con ellas a levantar mi vista como montaña
que atraviesa las nubes en Waras. Al atardecer, las rojas nubes se pintan con mi sangre derramada en mi tesoro.
Y yo las contemplo con mi pobre vestido de todos los colores, con el agua y el pan de mis ancestros bajo la nieve…
Me llaman aquella sin derecho a vivir en un lugar tranquilo, pero yo soy Fátima de Hazaristán.

Temo que la muerte no sólo llega con la dura nevada en Dai Kundi sino con los hombres de los ojos del mal fuego
que no saben de la compasión. Vuelo con la Gran Cigüeña y las raras especies de pájaros, pero los hombres
del mal fuego en los ojos no me dejan emigrar hacia la felicidad. Escucho la canción de mi bisabuela
a través del sendero peligroso y sigo esperando que florezca la perenne paz del Buda de Baymán.

Angelina Llongueras
Catalonia

Angelina Llongueras, PhD, is a poet, actress, playwright, director, professor, and researcher born in Barcelona and relocated to Chicago. Her credits include a two-year tour of Europe and Asia as lead actress in *Metamorfosis* by La Fura dels Baus. Her *Phoolan is Everyone*— participated in the Bogotá and Cali's Women's Theatre Festivals, in 2010, and in 2012 in the International Women Playwright's conference in Stockholm, Sweden.

Angelina has performed for film directors like Almodovar and Bardem, has directed "Pedro and the Captain by Benedetti" and Shakespeare's "Richard II", among others. Her play "El Cobert" (The Junk Room) won the finalist mention of the 14th April Prize for Theatre about Historical Memory in 2009.

She has taught courses and seminars in universities in the US, Mexico, France and Spain. Angelina is a member of the San Francisco Revolutionary Poets brigade.

Very recently, she was cast in "Shadow Town" by Her Story Theater in Chicago which will premiere in October 2013.

A POEM IN CATALAN FOR THE HAZARA PEOPLE

Do not let my name be erased from history(*)
Julia Conesa
"The Thirteen Roses"

Kamran, friend,

exiled friend,

from a lost community of people,

called Hazara,

in the center of Asia,

in the navel of the world,

in Afghanistan:

a community who is being massacred…

You write from Norway

crying,

and requesting

the poets of the world

to be distant voices,

who give presence,

to these silenced deaths,

perpetrated by both:

Talibans and Americans…

It is difficult for me

to place in the map

your rebellious people,

your mountain people,

agonizing,

whom I have seen only in pictures,

and who convey to me

the suffering of the honest ones,

the people with an innocent smile,

who still root themselves in the earth,

who are still a part

of their ancestral landscape,

who are a pulled out, cornered

animal species,

who do not understand the whys,

who do not know about money…

just like we ourselves

sad representatives

of the scattered,

exiled, uprooted

animal species

do not understand either,

even though we think

we are citizens of the world.

There had been a time,

not so long ago,

although it seems to have taken place
in another life,
when the world was big
and full of hope.

Today it has shrunk,
It has become ugly,
horrible!
and without being conscious of it,
it agonizes each day
side by side with the Hazara,
side by side with your people,
because every lost Hazara heartbeat
gives off a wave
that undoes its name and existence
and sinks us all a little bit more
in the slavery to the New Order
that can only be stopped by conscience.

The "Order" of the War Lords
who commit ongoing genocides
in buildings that are sunk
by flagrant exploitation,
and, with very modern weapons,
that are turned on
so as to erase
nomad peasant peoples,

shepherd people's

like yours,

like the Hazara,

the Quiché,

the Mapuche,

the Qom,

and so many others

whose names we do not even know

and who are being

literally

exterminated…

the last wise peoples,

the guardians…

Right this instant

my small voice

tells of you,

feels you,

listens to you,

and it has no tears left,

just the echo of an incessant scream

that wants to cross the mountains

and reach the sea

so as to be able to cry,

and cry,

and cry,

and cry,

without end…

(*)This quotation from Julia Conesa (in Spanish in the original, not in Catalan) appeared in her last letter to her family just before being executed by firing squad by the Franco fascists then in the government of Spain, for having helped people in danger of being murdered to escape.

"The Thirteen Roses" is the name that has been given to thirteen girls in Madrid who were executed all together on the same day, the majority of whom were minors, the eldest being 22 years old. Julia Conesa was one of them.

To be allowed to write her letter she was forced to "confess her sins" to a catholic priest. If they did not, their last letter was not given to their families.

POEMA EN CATALÀ PEL POBLE HAZARA

> *Que mi nombre no se borre de la historia*
> *Julia Conesa*
> *"Las Trece Rosas"*

Amic Kamran,

amic exiliat

d'un poble perdut,

anomenat Hazara,

al centre de l'Àsia,

al melic del món,

a l'Afghanistan:

un poble al que estan massacrant...

Escrius des de Noruega

plorant,

i demanant

als poetes del mon,

que siguem veus distants,

que donem presència

a aquestes morts silenciades,

i perpetrades,

per tots dos junts:

talibans i americans...

I m'és difícil
posar al mapa
la teva gent ferèstega,
gent de muntanya,
agonitzant,
a qui conec només per fotos,
i que em transmeten
el sofriment dels íntegres,
dels pobles de mirada innocent,
que encara s'arrelen a la terra,
que son encara part
del seu paisatge ancestral,
que són espècie animal
arrancada i acorralada
que no entén res dels per quès,
que no coneix els diners...

com tampoc no ho entenem nosaltres,
tristos representants
de les espècies animals
dispersades,
exilades,
i desarrelades,
encara que pensem
que sóm ciutadans del món

Hi havia un temps

no tant llunyà
tot i que sembla haver tingut lloc
en una altra vida,
que el mon era gran
i tenia esperança.

Avui s'ha empetitit,
s'ha tornat lleig,
horrible!
i sense ser-ne conscient,
agonitza cada dia
al costat dels Hazara,
al costat del teu poble,
perquè cada batec hazara perdut
emet una ona silenciosa
que en desfà nom i existència,
i ens ensorra un xic més a tots
en l'esclavatge al Nou Ordre
que només pot deturar la consciència.

L' "Ordre" dels Senyors de la Guerra
que cometen genocidis constants,
en edificis que ensorra
una explotació flagrant,
i, amb armes ben modernes,
que estan engegant
per anar esborrant

pobles pagesos i nòmades,
pobles de pastors,
com el teu,
com els Hazara,
els Quiché,
els Mapuche,
els Qom,
i tants altres
que ni el nom en sabem
als qui estan literalment
exterminant...

els darrers pobles savis,
els guardians....

En aquest instant
la meva veu petita
us està dient,
us està sentint,
us està escoltant,
i no li queden llàgrimes
sinó l'eco d'un crit incessant
que vol travessar les muntanyes
i arribar al mar
per poder plorar,
i plorar,
i plorar,

i plorar...

sense parar....

May 5th 2013

Aju Mukhopadhyay
India

Aju Mukhopadhyay, Pondicherry, India, is an award winning bilingual poet, author of fiction and non-fiction works and critic. He has authored thirty books and has received several poetry awards, besides other honors from India and abroad. Many of his works have been translated in Indian and foreign languages and anthologized. There are eight books which include discussions on his poetry. He has written essays on more than forty scholarly books on literature and allied subjects like Nature and Environment. Aju has been in the editorial boards of some serious literary journals. He has participated in thirty national and international literary and tribal life conferences. A member of the Research Board of Advisors of the American Biographical Institute, he has travelled across Asia, Europe, America, and Africa.

His important books include:
Sri Aurobindo's Ideal of Freedom and Human Unity (Essays), *Sri Aurobindo: The Yogi of Divine Life* (Philosophy and biography), *The World of Sri Aurobindo's Creative Literature* (Literary), *The Mother Of All Beings* (Biography), *The Witness Tree* (Poems), *In Celebration of Nature* (Poems), *The Paper Boat* (Poems), *Insect's Nest and Other Poems* (Poems), *The Moments of Life* (Short Stories), *In Train* (novel)

IN REASONABLE SUPPORT OF THE HAZARA PEOPLE

Though born differently in shape size and quality

all living beings are born with equal birth rights

to be taken care of by the Mother Earth;

none has the right to dwarf or cull others

unless it is Nature's spontaneous action

in helping species and individuals

to maintain harmony in death and survival.

Humans too are born with their unequal inherent capacities

but born with equal rights to share

earth water fire space and air.

Tribal life is one of the beginnings of human social life;

some people love to remain in their pristine past

some go ahead to make the most of natural resources

in their makeshift civilization

but humans have no right over the others

to extinguish them for self-interest or self-assertion.

All religions are self-divisive, self-assertive;

curbing women's rights and sectarian deadly fights

destroying revered monuments of the other religions with hate

are the works of the philistines who live in every age

the offspring of the sterile religious rocky crust;

with that none has the right to compel others

to comply with their faiths; it is their ill-begotten ideas

to bring others to their fold religious.

Hazaras are a distinct ethnic group, may be with their
Mongolian-Buddhist past, linguistic touch
with the Turk, Persians or the other Islamic sects;
they cherish a forgotten idea, keep a bygone thought
some forgotten mantras vibrate in their hearts
but true it is in the recorded history of hundreds of years
that their birth place is Central Asian Afghanistan;
they're now relocated in other countries due to persecution and fear
though they've every right to live in their land as live the others.
It is the voice of the Poets voice of Peace voice of Love
for the Hazara people, appealing to all who have been
so far persecuting them, appealing to all humans throughout
the globe to put a stop to it mainly because we're humans;

not dogs who chase and kill the other dogs that enter their territory.
In wonderment we observe that the persecutors are
from their own land, sufferers suffer within their own boundary;
after aeons of development of civilizations
how men can be inferior to dogs?
Rise up brothers to forget and embrace the brothers
be humane, not just logs.

THE VICTIMS OF THE EVIL FORCES

Religion at its heart is a seeking

For the beyond, adoring the lord

Neither a social code

Nor a relationship with the woman;

In most religions and religious scriptures

There have been interpolations

Interferences by the ineligible intruders

At later stages of their growth

That complicated their future roles in human life.

The founders of great religions

Which were formulated usually after their departure

Were guided by the divine voices

But there seems to be some other cases

Where the beginner were guided

By the Satanic Evil forces and their voices

Giving birth to all distortions, terrorism and destructions;

Conflict continues in such groups of religions,

Divided into many, among them and beyond them.

While religion is expected to be a source of higher life

History teaches the contrary, that it is full of strife.

The earth is still burning at different places

Indicating mostly the same groups' internecine presence.

Hazara people seems to be the victims of such
Feud, jealousy and ever increasing wrath
Produced by the perverse and misguided belief
Contrary to the religious path.
The hatred and fire spread
To defile the Buddhist heritage,
Strangle and shoot the student
Who wished to grow in knowledge,
To torture and pierce with multiple bullets brutally
The woman writer and social worker
Coming from a different country
Working to bring light to their society.
The whole world is pin pointing the culprits
For Such things cannot go unnoticed.

Instead of keeping silence or supporting
Tacitly such dastardly acts
Let the sane voices from such groups
Rise up to deny the heritage of such falsehood.
Let them come forward to emend their religion
In conformity with the higher moral and spiritual light
For reform and revision are the processes of life
To usher in a new age of honesty and Integrity bright
In keeping with the peaceful human right.

Ban'ya Natsuishi
Japan

Natsuishi was born in Japan in 1955 and studied at Tokyo University where he received a Masters of Arts in Comparative Literature and Culture. He is prominent as an international promoter of haiku writing and translation. He published fourteen haiku collections, including *Earth Pilgrimage* (1998), *Flying Pope* (2008) and *Black Card* (2012), seven collected haiku critical studies, including *Poetics of Haiku* (1983) and *Haiku Juomujin* (2010, co-authored with Sayumi Kamakura), and edited ten volumes of multilingual haiku anthologies, the latest *World Haiku 2013: No. 9* (2013).

Natsuishi's haikus were translated into about thirty languages, including English, French, Italian, Lithuanian, and Spanish. He has authored and co-authored many overseas publications, beginning with *A Future Waterfall* (USA, 1999 & 2004), *Flying Pope: 127 Haiku* (India, 2008) and *Concentric Circles* (Serbia, 2009), *Turquoise Milk: 500 Haikus from the Japanese* (USA, 2011), *Modern Japanese Haiku* (India, 2012), among others. In 2002 he won the Hekigodo Kawahigashi Prize; and in 2008 he won the AZsacra International Poetry Award.

Currently Natsuishi works as a Professor at Meiji University, and is the publisher of the international haiku quarterly "Ginyu," as well as the co-founder & director of the World Haiku Association and Tokyo Poetry Festival Committee.

HAIKU FOR HAZARA PEOPLE
ハザラの人々への俳句

1

Thrown from Jesus to Buddha

my right year

works well

イエスから釈迦へ投げられ右耳働く

2

A sorrow for the future

thrust into

the blue sky of fear

恐怖の青空に突き刺さる未来への悲しみ

3

This seed is a bomb

then

a perfect musical note

種は爆弾そして完全な音符

4

Getaway—
a moondial
at the bottom of a desert

逃亡や砂漠の底に月時計

5

If despair is a fountain,

love is

a pigeon

絶望が噴水ならば愛は鳩

Julio Pavanetti
Uruguay/Spain

Julio Pavanetti (Montevideo, Uruguay, 1954) is a writer, a poet, and a cultural manager who belongs to the generation of young people who suffered under the rigors of his country's military dictatorship. Facing a very difficult socio-political situation, he decided to leave Uruguay and in 1977 settled permanently in Benidorm, Spain.

- Co-founder and current President of the "Liceo Poético de Benidorm"
- Honorary Vice President of the "World Organization of Poets, Writers, and Artists".
- Consul of the "International World Poets Movement" for Foreign Uruguay.
- Cultural Delegate for Uruguay of "Hispano-American Union of Writers".
- Official representative in Alicante of the "Cultural Movement aBrace" establish in Brazil and Uruguay.
- Member of the "Association of Spanish Writers and Artists".
- Member of the "World Network of Writers in Spanish".
- Member of the "World Poetry Movement".

Pavanetti has participated in several international festivals of poetry representing either Spain or Uruguay. His bibliography includes four books and four anthologies. His works have been included in fifteen anthologies.

His poems have been translated into English, Italian, Arabic, Romanian, Portuguese, Croatian, German, and Dutch and have been published on innumerable national and international newspapers and literary magazines, both in digital and printed format.

THE VOICE OF ALL OF US

The Hazara people's voice
is the cry of the poet
exclaiming verse by verse
that opens their eyes and ears
to the suffering of people
who they are seeking to erase
until they remove their skin.

The Hazara people's voice
is the force of the poet
joining his pen to other pens
to plant their looks
of green branches
with their fruits of hope
that would stop the pain.

The Hazara people's voice
stands besides the poet
to reclaim the world
to curb the massacres
no more blood running
and that people are not pushed

to the pits of oblivion.

The Hazara people's voice
belongs to all of us
poets who fight
with pen and word
for human rights
for peace and justice
for a free world.

The Hazara people's voice
is mine and yours.
Let us unite all voices
in a single, powerful scream
that shake the foundations
of all the powerful men
until they bite the dust.

31/3/2013

LA VOZ DE TODOS

La voz del pueblo Hazara
es el grito del poeta
exclamando verso a verso
que abre sus ojos y oídos
al sufrimiento de un pueblo
al que pretenden borrar
hasta quitarles la piel.

La voz del pueblo Hazara
es la fuerza del poeta
que unce su pluma a otras plumas
para plantar sus miradas
de frondosas ramas verdes
con sus frutos de esperanza
que detengan el dolor.

La voz del pueblo Hazara
se alza junto al poeta
para reclamarle al mundo
que se frenen las masacres
que ya no corra más sangre
y que no se empuje a un pueblo
a las fosas del olvido.

La voz del pueblo Hazara
es la de todos nosotros
los poetas que luchamos
con la pluma y la palabra
por los derechos humanos
por la paz y la justicia
por un mundo en libertad.

La voz del pueblo Hazara
es la mía y es la tuya.
Unamos todas las voces
en un solo y potente grito
que sacuda los cimientos
de todos los poderosos
hasta que besen el polvo.

31/3/2013

Gertrude Fester
Rwanda/ South Africa

A feminist activist for most of her life, Gertrude has been privileged to have diverse positions. She was a Member of Parliament in the African National Congress (ANC) and led the first democratic parliament until 1999. Like many others in parliament, she has also been a political prisoner in Apartheid South Africa and kept in solitary confinement for almost 5 months.

One bonus of being left without books or writing material she acknowledges, was being challenged to 'write' a play in her head as a survival mechanism. She has performed this play, *The Spirit Shall Not Be Caged*, in various countries. She has been charged with treason along with thirteen others. These charges were withdrawn after a 3-year trial when the ANC was unbanned in 1990 and Nelson Mandela was freed. Other accomplishments include being a Commissioner on Gender Equality, a constitutional position mandated to promote, educate, and monitor gender equality in South Africa. . She is passionate about education and taught for about twenty years, fifteen of those training teachers.

Gertrude has a PhD from the London School of Economics. She has published both fiction and non-fiction, focusing mostly on women's lives. If she had more time, she would spend it doing performance poetry. She received the Hammet - Hellman Human Rights Prize for Writers in 1997. In 2001, she was the Wynona Lipman Chair for Women Political leaders at the Center for American Women and Politics, Rutgers University, New Jersey and Distinguished Visiting Professor at the African and Afro-American Studies Department at Washington University in St. Louis, USA.

Currently her research and activism explore the root causes of violence against women and citizenship for vulnerable groups, focusing on the influences of culture and religion. She also is doing archival research on the lives of slave and First Nation women in South Africa, her ancestors. She is a Professor of Transitional Justice and Gender Equality, at the Centre for Gender, Culture and Development, Institute of Education, Kigali, Rwanda. She is currently working on a manuscript featuring young Rwandans' writings on Transitional Justice mainstreaming gender. Most of her publications, both fiction and non-fiction, are on women's lives.

HOPE FOR THE HAZARAS

How do i use the power of my pen to highlight your pain?
How do i weave words of wonder to give you hope for your homeland?
How to i volume my voice in concern and anger about your plight?
How do i dance my activist gyrations to garner support for your freedom?
How do I pray a prayer of intercession for the facilitation of your independence?

I will pen a poem in solidarity with poets from all corners of the world
Exposing the lies spun by your oppressors surrounding your lives
Together we will weave a symphony of protests at the treatment you get
Sing a song of hope and
I will write with wild words shouting of your pain and plight
I will gyrate and dance a dance of freedom,
Each movement a moment towards confidence, a dance of optimism,
Swiveling swings of sunshine
Turning the tides
That the powerless will free themselves from the yoke of oppression

21 April 2013

HOMAGE TO THE HAZARA PEOPLE

I sing a sad song … so many people still suffer

But also
I sing a song of praise for the beauty of nature, the mountains in their majesty,
the rivers running wildly riveting over rocks and meandering mindlessly midsts reeds and ....
I sing a sad song … so many people still suffer

I sing a song of woe
and wonder when all the pain of the Hazara people will pass
I still sing a sad song … so many people suffer

I sing a song of freedom for the Hazara people
I sing a song of inspiration
The Hazaras may not lose hope

I sing a song of solace in expectation that soon a solution like the sun will rise

I shout a slogan of anger
I swing of spear of revolution
I mobilise masses to make miracles
To fight oppressors

To tell the story of their pained past.

I weave these words
I sing these songs to tell a story of the Hazara past
A past of slavery, exploitation,
Dehumanisation and pain
But also their power not to remain victims…

I write a page of protest prompting the past pain not to recur...
I sing a song of freedom for the Hazara people
I sing a song of inspiration
Our Hazara sisters and brothers do not lose hope
I sing a song of solace in expectation that soon a solution shall sprout forth
As surely as the sun shall rise.

23 May 2013

Jack Hirschman
Revolutionary Poets Brigade, San Francisco, USA

Jack Hirschman was the fourth Poet Laureate of the City of San Francisco (2006-2009) and he is the current Poet in Residence with the Friends of the San Francisco Public Library. He coordinates with the Friends of the San Francisco Public Library to organize the San Francisco International Poetry Festival. He also curates weekly readings of politically engaged poets at Readers Bookstore in San Francisco. Jack's own works include more than one hundred published books, sixty of which are translations of other poets' work. His magnum opus is a lengthy book of poems called *The Arcanes* published in the English language in Italy by Multimedia Edizioni.

SIX HAIKUS

1

not simply for the
people who speak hazaragi
but for all people

2

in afghanistan,
italistan, turkestan,
newyorkistan and

3

all who suffer with

guns to their mouths, to their heads,

in the sniper aim,

4

we must bring the war

criminals to their knees by

finally the new class

5

party of the poor
people of this sad world
and create the communist

6

revolution that
has never before appeared
on the horizon!

Iztok Osojnik
Slovenia

Iztok Osojnik was born in 1951 in Ljubljana, Slovenia. He is a poet, fiction writer, literary scientist, essayist, editor, translator, artist, tour director, and a mountain climber. His many professions took him all around the world. He was a trendsetter in his youth and a co-founder of the prankish *sous-realisme* movement.

Iztok graduated with a degree in Comparative Literature from the University of Ljubljana (1977) and participated in postgraduate studies at Osaka Gaidai University (1980-82). In 2011, he completed his PhD at the University of Primorska in Koper. He is the former director of the International literary festival Vilenica and currently organizes The Golden Boat international poetry translation Workshop. So far, he has published twenty-seven collections of poetry, five novels, and four volumes of essays on literature, anthropology, and philosophy (in the Slovenian language).

Iztok has published four books of poetry in English: *Alluminations* (City Gallery of Arts of Ljubljana), a collection of poetry *And Some Things Happen for the First Time* (Modry Peter, Canada 2001),

Mister Today (Jacaranda Press, California 2004), *New, and Selected Poems* (Sampark, New Delhi 2010) and *Elsewhere* (Pighog Press, Brighton 2011).

His poems and essays were translated and published in twenty-five languages. He was awarded several national and international literary awards, most lately with the prestigious international award KONS 2011.

FOR THE HAZARA PEOPLE

yes, i remember ban-de-amir and bamiyan
the great buddha in the sandstone cavern
nearly 40 years ago
I remember sands, hills, mountains, snows, towns, adobe houses
I remember late afternoons, a shining moon, and still valleys of almond trees
I remember songs of muezzins and village men with bows and arrows on the edge of a village shooting at a target
I remember different times of the year i travelled through
I remember glittering eyes of beautiful women and children
the most beautiful in the whole world
and kind and sometimes suspicious looks by men
the night when they invited us to a dinner
men with dark eyes and with long knives which they laid down besides them when we sat down and started to feast
and later when they brought watermelons and a nargila, their dark, glittering eyes
in the darkness lightened by candles only
I never knew what that was all about
why us, why did they come to pick us up in the modest hotel
brought us to dinner, not very much was spoken, a whispering here
a quick word there, that strange eating in silence
but some kind of deep sympathy was established that night between us

Mister Today (Jacaranda Press, California 2004), *New, and Selected Poems* (Sampark, New Delhi 2010) and *Elsewhere* (Pighog Press, Brighton 2011).

His poems and essays were translated and published in twenty-five languages. He was awarded several national and international literary awards, most lately with the prestigious international award KONS 2011.

FOR THE HAZARA PEOPLE

yes, i remember ban-de-amir and bamiyan

the great buddha in the sandstone cavern

nearly 40 years ago

I remember sands, hills, mountains, snows, towns, adobe houses

I remember late afternoons, a shining moon, and still valleys of almond trees

I remember songs of muezzins and village men with bows and arrows on the edge of a village shooting at a target

I remember different times of the year i travelled through

I remember glittering eyes of beautiful women and children

the most beautiful in the whole world

and kind and sometimes suspicious looks by men

the night when they invited us to a dinner

men with dark eyes and with long knives which they laid down

besides them when we sat down and started to feast

and later when they brought watermelons and a nargila, their dark, glittering eyes

in the darkness lightened by candles only

I never knew what that was all about

why us, why did they come to pick us up in the modest hotel

brought us to dinner, not very much was spoken, a whispering here

a quick word there, that strange eating in silence

but some kind of deep sympathy was established that night between us

mass murdering, torturing, massacres, crimes against nature and humanity and against all
living creatures? what does it cry out that sparkle in the eyes of the nameless girl on the bus from band-de-amir to kabul in february 1978,
what does it tell
what does it stand for?
in the dark light of the horrendous abyss of endless crime

Erling Kittelsen
Norway

Kittelsen had his debut as a poet in 1970. He has since published several poetry cycles and collections, as well as fables, dramatic works and translations of poetry.

He is known for his dialogues, partly with colleagues and partly in the work with the translation of poetry from distant languages in relation to the Nordic language area like Arabian, Persian, Korean, Latvian, and Sumerian. He also has poetical dialogue with the most ancient poetical traditions in the Nordic Countries – the Old Norse Poetic Edda where at first he translates the old text and then presents a contemporary literary answer.

Erling is known as a writer who renews language, a poet, and a storyteller. He is a writer who moves in non-traditional ways, both with the language in his books and dramatic works and his literary activity through events and happenings. His last play was translated and performed several times in the Middle East.

Erling has received several literary prices, amongst them The Aschehoug Prize (awarded on a binding recommendation by the Norwegian Critics Organization) and The DoblougPrize (awarded by the Swedish Academy).

HUMAN- HAZARA

They wanted to have them from a distance
and gladly love them
if they could travel long
like waking up a dead,
gotten part in their insights
or taken the most beautiful among them
or listened to a singer
that hit larynx like a string
bringing in another sound
another pause

didn't fit to have them here,
nor the yurt they were living in
the belief belonged to the enemy
why were they sometimes in the midst
that mountain doesn't fit in here
that mountain lets itself to be taken down
like a tent, they learned
then they may disappear

the mountain takes down like tent
the tent rises like mountain

MENNESKE-HAZARA

På avstand ville de ha dem
og gjerne elske dem
hvis de kunne reist langt
som å vekke opp en død
og fått del i deres innsikt
eller tatt den vakreste blant dem
eller lyttet til en sanger som slo
strupehodet som en streng
hente inn en annen lyd
annen pause

passet ikke helt å ha dem her
heller ikke jurten som de bodde i
troen var helst fiendens
hvorfor var de midt iblant
det fjellet passer ikke her
det fjellet lar seg rigge ned
som et telt, lærte de
da kan de vel dra bort

fjellet rigges ned som duk
duken rigges opp som fjell

Obediah Michael Smith
Bahamas

Obediah Michael Smith was born on New Providence, in the Bahamas, in 1954 and has published seventeen books of poetry.

At University of Miami and University of the West Indies, Cavehill, Barbados, he participated in writers workshops facilitated by Lorna Goodison, Earl Lovelace, Grace Nichols, Merle Collins, and Mervyn Morris. He attended Memphis State University, 1973 to 1976 and majored in Speech & Drama and Biology.

Obediah has a Bachelor of Arts Degree, in Dramatics and Speech, from Fisk University. He has lived and has studied French, in Paris, France. His poems, in English, are included in literary journals and anthologies throughout the Caribbean, in the USA and in England and his poems, translated into Spanish, are included in anthologies in Colombia, in Mexico, in Peru, in Venezuela and in Spain. He has studied Spanish at Universidad de Costa Rica.

HAZARISTAN

find yourself in some
geographical location
on earth, coupled with its climate
and you have to adapt: eek out life

wherever the sky is though
there is protection
and wherever water flows
life is possible

what is amazing though
is to be making the most
of little or nothing
and along come those

at times from the skies
where there are eyes
watching over us
where rain falls from

along come forces against us
to break our earthenware pots
and jugs and in addition, our heads

unable to avoid

having to prepare for war
as we live in peace

however little we live upon
however little we have to exist
if we do not clutch tight
cling to what we have

if you do not fight
or are not prepared to
we can be reduced
to dead, to dirt, to earth

we could be relieved of breath
and death and no more can remain

sweet life and love recalled
and we struggle to survive
to sustain our kind
our time on earth

not prepared, just like that,
to be a people that was
to become extinct

we battle the elements
as well as our fellowman

the stuff of which we are made

as sturdy as history

what troubles orbiting planets
have to face to stay on course

that same law inside us
to orbit on and on
to continue to be

                                                        10:06 p.m. 19.07.13

HAZARISTAN AMONG RUGGED MOUNTAINS

"You fuckers!"
you want to say
and hurl a hand grenade
right back at your attackers

must be armed to the teeth
must be ready for war

but what has a poet but a pen with ink
what has a poet but a head of letters

must a poet make war with these
first the words, then the deeds

these are not times to fool around in
we are not people to fool around with

blood within our veins, our arteries, running
running as long as the rivers
along which we live

rivers making valleys

among these mountains

cutting rock, cutting glass
crystal, diamond, a part of us
a part of these

tested, tried, made wet, made dry

the hot, the chill, the crack of ice
the crackling fires upon which we cook
about which we sit, we reminisce

tell stories of old - some new tales

when tragedy struck
hot tears flowed, our women cried

their breast milk too
nipples in young babies' mouths

sucking, supping, life to live
war arriving over the hills

fathers die, grinning skulls
nothing at all to laugh about

no peace in this world

no piece of this world
without a fight, without contest

rubble, ruin
of what hands built carefully
of what took years

in an instant, in the blast of war

to heaven to cry out
to the Almighty we wail

to the might that is mightier
than any man-made

the whirling planets
the spinning earth, the orderly
orbiting of the universe

chaos comes, chaos goes
what is eternal
we are part of–
we are made of

the harmony, the song
the singing birds
the changing seasons

winter, summer
autumn, spring
unalterable routine

steady, rotating
orbiting earth

ride we're on
will not be thrown off

who wage war
no more than ants
in the vastness of the universe

when measured against
how endless eternity is

we will abide beside these rivers
among these mountains
as long as time is

defying the weather
the white-cold winters
and whatever other trials
whatever other troubles beset us

brave what threatens
what's treacherous

afterwards, we smile again
we smile again, after all

11:49 p.m. 27.11.13

Bina Sarkar Ellias
India

Bina Sarkar Ellias is the founder, editor, designer, and publisher of International Gallerie, the global arts and ideas journal encouraging understanding of cultural diversity. She is also a curator, poet, and fiction writer. Bina received a Fellowship from the Asia Leadership Fellow Program and Japan Foundation, 2007, for research and development of the project, "Unity in Diversity: Envisioning Community Building in Asia and Beyond," the Times Group Yami Women Achievers' award, 2008, and the FICCI/FLO 2013 award for excellence in her work.

like
trees axed
by ignorance
and savage hate,
sundered, slain
Hazaras flung afar
forsaken by
kin of kin
unite.

unite

Hazaras.
arise, claim
your universe
unite, in one belief
as do comrades
in brotherhood
and sisterhood
that we will
overcome.

unite.

we are
all Hazara
black, white,

yellow, brown,
the blood in our veins
a shared red, let
compassion flow
before we're
dust, before
we're dead.

unite.

we will
weed out
the blight that
killed the right
to equality. we will
seed anew the invincible
in brotherhood
in sisterhood.
we will keep
aflame our
heroic
faith.

unite.

just
as rivers
meet, as sky

and sea converge
as clouds touch earth
with seasonal rain
just as all is one
and one is all
let tolerance
prevail.

a hymn for Hazaras
a hymn for humanity

when racism is indictable
when unity is sine qua non
when hearts open wide for all
when wisdom dawns

only then shall we be civilized
only then shall hope be realized

you and I are ever one
let us claim our birthright
let us all be Hazara,
let us all unite.

Raúl Henao
Colombia

RAÚL HENAO: (Cali, Colombia, 1944). Raul has lived in Venezuela, México and the United States. He has published the following books: *Combate del Carnaval y la Cuaresma* (1973); *La Parte del León* (Caracas, 1978); *El Bebedor Nocturno* (Poems in prose for which he obtained a Second Prize in the National Poetry Concurse Eduardo Cote Lamus, Cúcuta, 1977); *El Dado Virgen* (Caracas, 1980); *Sol Negro* (Medellín, 1985); *El Partido del Diablo, Poesía y Crítica* (Medellín, 1989); *El Virrey de los Espejos* (Medellín, 1996); *La Vida a la Carta / Life a la Carte* (1998); *La belleza del diablo* (Madrid, 1999); *La doble estrella. El surrealism en iberoamérica* (Ensayos, Medellín.2010); *La verdad en el vino* (Antología, Bogotá.2012).

To him, the most important Ibero-American and world anthologies, are: *Parasurrealist Latin American Poets* (Honolulu, Hawaii, 1982); *The Beloit Poetry Journal – New Latin American Poets* (Wisconsin, EE.UU., 1982); *Nordic and Latin American Surrealist Poets* (Sweden, 1984); *Poetry of Spain and The Americas* (Puerto Rico, 1992); *Hispano-American Poets for The Third Millennium* (México, 1993); *Anthology of Latin American Haiku* (Sao Pablo, Brazil, 1993); *The Daedalus Book of Surrealism / The Myth of the World* (London, 1994); *Das Surrealistische Gedicht* (Frankfurt am Main, Germany, 2001) and *Poesys de Dragoste* / Antología Festivalul International Noptile de Poezie de la Curtea de Arges (Romania, 2001).

His poems have been partially translated into English, French, German, Portuguese, Rumanian and Swedish.

HAZARA

Hazara: Towers and white tents in the distance, in the middle of the steppes and deserts of Hazaristán ... halfway of the Silk Road. Village of all deaths and revivals, village of all exiles and protests, that bring on muleback or camel the search of his destiny or identity.

The bear and the eagle with his necklace, have laid siege to your cities but have not been heeded by the courage of your people who shields a single verse of the Holy Qur'an (Sura 9, 51).

"This will never happen to us but what God has decreed. He is our protector "

That neither Abd el Rahman and Mullah Omar, in his time and at the time, using the looting and strength, treachery and outrage, they got refute or deny.

Hazara: village of the steppes and Hazaristán dusty asphalt, strain nomadic Turkish and Mongol, of whom inherited in the past the worship of images of the Buddhas of Bamiyan: Let your people get off the thirst of the war with the heavenly potion of peace, tribal grudges with love of neighbor, and finally unite, tolerance faith, hope, and humanity's future.

Medellín, May. 2013.

Translation: Elizabeth Gallego Montoya

HAZARA

HAZARA : Torres y tiendas blancas a lo lejos, a mitad de las estepas y desiertos del Hazaristan… a mitad de camino de la ruta de la seda. Pueblo de todas las muertes y resurrecciones, de todos los exilios y diásporas que traen a lomo de mula o camello la búsqueda del propio destino o identidad.

El oso y el águila acollarada han puesto cerco a tus ciudades pero no han conseguido doblegar el coraje de tus gentes a quienes escuda una sola aleya del Al Cur´anu-l- Karim-

"Jamás nos acontecerá sino lo que Dios nos haya decretado. Él es nuestro protector" (Sura 9, 51)

Que ni Abd el Rahman ni el Mullah Omar, en su hora y momento, haciendo uso del saqueo y la fuerza, la alevosía y el desmán consiguieron desmentir o negar.

HAZARA pueblo de las estepas y solares polvorientos del Hazaristan, estirpe nómada del turco y el mogol, de quienes heredaste en el pasado el culto a las imágenes de los Budas del Bamiyan. Que tu pueblo consiga apagar la sed de la guerra con la pócima paradisíaca de la paz, los rencores tribales con el amor al prójimo y aunar finalmente la fe a la tolerancia, la esperanza a la humanidad del porvenir.

Anne Waldman
USA

Anne Waldman is the author of forty books including most recently *Manatee/Humanity* and *Gossamurmur (Penguin Poets 2013)* and the award winning anti-war feminist *IOVIS TRILOGY: Colors in the Mechanism of Concealment*. She is a co-founder, with Allen Ginsberg, of the Jack Kerouac School at Naropa University.

SPEAK FOR THE HAZARA

Speak for them
speak for the Hazara
enigmatic people
travel back in blue time
with mysterious origin- Mongel?
constructed the Bamiyan Buddhas?

speak for the Hazara
caught in the tangle of geo-political tragedy
speak for those who resist
machinations of power on all sides
caught in a treacherous web
losing heritage, sweet custom,
land, language…bright indomitable spirit

speak out for those who resist
their own obliteration

is the only answer a turn of weapon
or a "deal" of lucre?
may the world be held accountable
and mount a response to
stop all bloodshed

wake up
speak out for the Hazara…

Nguyen Quang Thieu
Vietnam

Nguyen Quang Thieu was born February 13, 1957 in Ha Tay province (now Hanoi). He is the Vice Chairman of The Association of Vietnamese Writers. The First Deputy to the General Secretary of Afro-Asian Writers' Union.

Thieu began writing in 1983 and published ten collections of poems, sixteen books of prose, three books of translation, two plays, and ten film scripts and over 300 essays and articles. Thieu's poems and short stories were published in the USA, Australia, Norway, France, Poland, Sweden, Japan, Korea, Venezuela, Colombia, Taiwan, Thailand, Ireland, and Indonesia. Thieu also paints. His first exhibition of oil paintings was held in The National Museum of Art in Hanoi in 2005.

LAST NIGHT A HAZARA BABY WAS BORN

In the darkness of the daybreak, I heard
The scream and I saw
The sad insomniac people who were sitting motionless
with one question
About their Hazara Nation

The wind was still blowing over their houses
And the river was still flowing through the fields
They have carried the question
of the sad insomniac Hazzara people
to my peaceful house and woken me up.

Last night there were some Hazara people
who left this world forever
But a dream was still hanging over
their coffins. A dream about a harvest,
about a fruit season, about a peaceful dinner
and about a story that was told but not to be broken off by a bullet

But from a thick darkness seems not to be erased
A cry of a new-born baby resounded
A citizen of Hazara was born
With his tiny hands that hold all power of life
And his open eyes

Were looking straight in the darkness
That is covering his Nation.

That baby was born from a sorrowful history
From a mother who carries a dream as if carrying a fetus
And walking in fears, in blood, in tears
In unreasonable deaths along the roads
Full of killers

Last night the human faced devils were dancing with guns
On the bloody road to the Hazara people's dream
And last night a Hazara baby was born to state
The undying Declaration of his Nation once more.

Timo Berger
Germany

Timo Berger, born 1974 in Stuttgart, lives in Berlin where he works as journalist, cultural manager, and translator from Spanish and Portuguese to German.

He writes poems and short stories. He is the co-founder of the latinamerican poetry festival Latinale, which is annual event since 2006.

IN THE EAST

For the Hazara

In the east

I stepped on sand

sometime

and I thought about

people

who passed through

this place:

traders

commanding camel caravans

bags

full of silk, salt

and spices;

preachers

spreading

his creed;

explorers,

astrolabe

under the arm

and the entrance to the desert

on their backs

a plain

prima facie

undefined

whose boundaries
are unthinkable to me,
I do not know the tricks
to draw water
on dry land,
protect myself from the sun,
the cold night
and decipher
the past and present
remains of the inhabitants
of this wasteland,
I hardly know
that in the middle
of this violent
country
Until recently
there was something
as a peaceful
island
a rock
now
at sea
beaten
by unassigned storms
by the finger of Zeus,
while we listen
shots, explosions

and some dead

floating in the imperative

current

not seen

from my window

overlooking a grove

in the heart

of a bourgeois

neighborhood

six thousand

kilometers

away.

EN EL ESTE

para los hazara

En el este

pisé arena

alguna vez

y pensé

en las personas

que pasaron

por este lugar:

comerciantes

al mando de caravanas

de camellos, bolsos

llenos de seda, sal

y especies;

predicadores

diseminando

su credo;

exploradores,

astrolabio

bajo el brazo

y la entrada al desierto

a sus espaldas

una planicie

a primera vista

indefinida,

cuyos confines
me son impensables
no sé los trucos
para extraer agua
en tierra seca,
protegerme del sol,
del frío nocturno
y decifrar
los vestigios
de los habitantes
pasados y presentes
de este páramo,
apenas sé
que en el medio
de este país
violento
hasta hace poco
existía algo
como una isla
pacífica
un peñasco
que ahora
en alta mar
es golpeado
por las tormentas
no asignadas
por el dedo de Zeus,

mientras se escuchan
tiros, detonaciones
y algunos muertos
flotan en la imperiosa
corriente
que no se ve
desde mi ventana
que da a una arboleda
en el corazón
de un barrio
burgués
a seis mil
kilómetros
de distancia.

2 de abril 2013

Elsa Tió
Puerto Rico

The president of PEN Club of Puerto Rico, Elsa Tio was born in San Juan, Puerto Rico. She has won the National Poetry Prize twice. She started typing before knowing how to write.

Elsa just published the poetry collection *Palabras sin escolta*. She defended the culture and language, because she understands it is the highest mark of a country's identity. She is devoted to rescuing Salvador Tio from oblivion by publishing the posthumous works of his father, writer, comedian, and poet. She fervently believes poetry is the miracle of language.

HAZARA

People, owner of the mountains, the plains, the seeds,
the stars, they enslaved and decimated you,
then, the earth opened up like a halved pain ,
and rivers were filled with tears and skies with terror
infinite anguish began a relentless struggle
and it emerged a new song. E.T.

Your people suffer lethargy
of freshly cut plant
of fresh wound
newly mourned penalty
that continues to distress.

It appears in your eyes
an endless struggle
the dignity of your song
born between the mountains
in the flower of your culture
that pleases the roots
and pokes you in the chest
wherever you go.

You provoke us astonishment
a country that resists

in captivity and combat
hugging the horizon
between light and mystery.
.

I hate that they dig your death
as your blood irrigates
to destroy your history
to make your voice nomadic.
I love how your song resists,
your vocation for justice
how you agglutinates beauty
enduring the consciousness
the energy of your poems
in emotion and faith.

HAZARA

Dueña de las semillas y las estrellas , de las montañas ,y las llanuras lo esclavizaron y lo diezmaron. Entonces se abrió la tierra como un dolor que se parte en dos, sus ríos se colmaron de llanto, sus cielos de espanto y empezó una angustia infinita y una lucha sin tregua y surgió otro nuevo canto .E.T.

Tu pueblo sufre un letargo
de planta recién cortada
de herida recién abierta
de pena recién llorada
que no cesa de angustiar .

Se desprende en tu mirada
una lucha interminable
un viento que alza la voz
y se enrosca por tus cantos
que nacen entre las montañas,
por la flor de tu cultura
que enamora las raíces
y se te clava en el pecho
por donde quiera que vayas.

Nos provocas el asombro
 al ser patria que resiste

en cautiverio y combate.
entre la luz y el misterio

Odio como te labran la muerte
como se riega tu sangre
como destruyen tu historia.
y hacen nómada tu voz.

Amo como resiste tu canto,
 tu vocación de justicia
 como aglutinas belleza
la conciencia perdurable
la dignidad de tus versos
en la emoción de la fe .

Kamran Mir Hazar
Hazaristan

Kamran Mir Hazar is an exiled Hazara poet, journalist, activist and webmaster. He has published several poetry books including the anthology, *Poems for The Hazara* (125 poets from 68 countries), *The Cry Of A Mare About To Become A Butterfly* (poetry) and *Stream of the Dear.* He is also the author of the non-fiction book, *Censorship in Afghanistan*. Kamran is publisher and editor-in-chief of the on-line news site, *Kabul Press*.

His website is www.kamranmirhazar.com.

WITH HAIKU'S BODY
با پیکر هایکو
1

With Haiku's Body:
He followed the DNA path
from haplogroup J2 connected to T
the coldness of mountains ran through his veins!

با پیکر هایکو:

مسیر دی ان ای را پیمود!

از هپلو گروپ جی 2 به تی پیوند خورد!

سرمای کوهستان در رگ هایش دوید!

Con il corpo dell'Haiku:
Ha seguito il sentiero del DNA
Dall'aplogruppo J2 collegato al T
il freddo delle montagne scorre
attraverso le sue vene

2

With Haiku's Body:

Sometime they want to chain your hands and feet!

If necessary become a fish,

If necessary an elephant saved from extinction!

با پیکر هایکو:

گاه می خواهند دست و پایت را ببندند!

لازم شد ماهی باش؛ لازم شد یک فیل نجات یافته از انقراض

Con il corpo dell'Haiku:

A volte vogliono legare

le tue mani ed i piedi

se necessario

divieni pesce

de necessario un elefante

salvato dall'estinzione

3

With Haiku's Body:

Kandahar, Lashkargah, Herat, Maimana, Sheberghan, Baghlan,

Charikar, Kabul, Ghazni and Dai chopan

with a mountain range in between!

با پیکر هایکو:

قندهار, لشکرگاه, هرات, میمنه, شبرغان, بغلان, چاریکار, کابل, غزنی و دای چوپان

با رشته کوهی در بین!

Con il corpo dell'Haiku:

Kandahar, Lashkargah, Herat,

Maimana, Sheberghan, Baghlan,

Charikar, Kabul, Ghazni e Dai chopan

al centro

una catena di montagne

4

With Haiku's Body:
A Times journalist in Kolkata, October 1893 reports
Amir of Afghanistan has sold ten thousand Hazara captives as slaves!

با پیکر هایکو:
خبرنگار تایمز در کلکته: اکتبر 1893
امیر افغان ده هزار بندی هزاره را به عنوان برده فروخت!

Con il corpo dell'Haiku:
Un giornalista del Times
a Kolkata
nell'Ottobre del 1893
riporta:
l'emiro dell'Afghanistan ha venduto
diecimila schiavi Hazara

5

With Haiku's Body:
They captured my fertile land and today they grow the greatest part of the world opium!

با پیکر هایکو:

زمین های حاصل خیزم را گرفتند و امروز بیشترین خشخاش جهان را تولید می کنند!

Con il corpo dell'Haiku:
Hanno sequestrato la mia fertile terra
ed oggi vi coltivano
la maggior parte dell'oppio
del mondo

6

With Haiku's Body:

October 1893,

Amir of Afghanistan has gathered forty thousand tribesmen to kill the Hazara!

با پیکر هایکو:

اکتبر 1893،

امیر افغان، چهل هزار اطرافی را برای کشتن هزاره جمع کرد!

Con il corpo dell'Haiku:

Ottobre 1893,

l'emiro dell'Afghanistan ha radunato

quattromila uomini di una tribù

per uccidere gli Hazara

7

With Haiku's Body:

- what I like to smell, while traveling from Bamiyan to Kabul is apple,

not the Taliban infection that abides for three centuries

با پیکر هایکو:

وقتی از بامیان به کابل می روم،

دوست دارم بوی سیب به مشامم برسد

نه طالب متعفنی که سه قرن تکرار شده است!

Con il corpo dell'Haiku:
Ciò che amo sentire
viaggiando da Bamiyan a Kabul,
è l'odore delle mele
non l'infenzione talebana
che da tre secoli ristagna

8

With Haiku's Body:

Did they disappear us enough that we disappear us too?

با پیکر هایکو:

به اندازه ی کافی ما را گم نکرده اند که ما هم خودمان را گم کنیم؟

Con il corpo dell'Haiku:

Ci hanno fatto scomparire abbastanza da far sparire anche noi?

9

With Haiku's Body:

Who from Behsood, Daimirdad, Ghazni, Daikondi or your Bamiyan didn't taste the bitter Kuchi-taliban?

با پیکر هایکو:

کدام تان از بهسود، دایمیرداد، غزنی، دایکندی تا بامیان تان، مزه ی تلخ کوچی طالب را نچشیده است؟

Con il corpo dell'Haiku:

Chi da Behsood, Daimirdad, Ghazni, Daikondi

o dalla tua Bamiyan non ha mai assaggiato

il sapore amaro dei kuchi talebani?

10

With Haiku's Body:
They block your Bamiyan- Kabul road, stand in your way and say you should be beheaded.
They shoot you down, trample your body with horses and then they burn you!

با پیکر هایکو

راه بامیان کابل تان را می بندند؛ سر راهتان را می گیرند و می گویند تو سرت نباشد،

تیرباران شوی و با اسب بر جنازه ات بتازند و به آتشت بکشند!

Con il corpo dell'Haiku:
Bloccano la strada tra Bamiyan e Kabul
ti impediscono di passare e
dicono che dovresti essere decapitato.
Ti sparano, i loro cavalli calpestano il tuo corpo
ed infine danno fuoco al tuo cadavere

11

With Haiku's Body:

Aaaah,

they make their crime our crime.

as if we would burn ourselves with our own hands!

با پیکر هایکو:

هی هی

– جرم خودشان را جرم ما می کنند!

همین را کم داشتیم که بدست خودمان ما را بسوزانند!

Con il corpo dell'Haiku:

Aaaah,

Hanno fatto del loro crimine

il nostro crimine

come se ci fossimo bruciati

con le nostre stesse mani

12

With Haiku's Body:

We must behave wisely

First, deep breaths

Then deep into ourselves!

با پیکر هایکو:

خردمندانه رفتار کنیم

ابتدا چند نفس باز بکشیم

سپس در خودمان فرو رویم و عمیق شویم!

Con il corpo dell'Haiku:

Dobbiamo agire saggiamente

per prima cosa

un bel respiro

e poi giù

nel profondo di noi stessi

13

With Haiku's Body:

OK, now, they want to kill me!

If I go to my Urozgan via my Kandahar, I'm already dead.

From Ghazni they kill me every day!

با پیکر هایکو:

خب حالا من را می خواهند بکشند!

اگر بخواهم از قندهارم به ارزگانم بروم، کشته شده ام!

از غزنی که هر روز مرا می کشند!

Con il corpo dell'Haiku:

Va bene, vogliono uccidermi

se passo da Kandahar per raggiungere

la mia Urozgan

sono già morto

da Ghazni invece

mi uccidono ogni giorno

14

With Haiku's Body:
I open Google maps in front of me.
Where is my fatherland,
is there a place for me?

با پیکر هایکو:
گوگل مپس را پیش رویم باز می کنم!
سرزمین من کجاست و آیا جایی برای زیستن در سرزمینم دارم؟

Con il corpo dell'Haiku:
Apro Google Maps di fronte a me
Dov'è la mia patria?
Esiste un posto per me?

15

With Haiku's Body:
I must care
for my almond trees,
work hard,
and if there is security,
sell almonds in Kabul!

با پیکر هایکو:
من باید به بادام هایم برسم!
باید سخت کار کرده و اگر امنیتی بود آن را در کابل سودا کنم!

Con il corpo dell'Haiku:
Devo prendermi cura
dei miei alberi di mandorlo,
lavorare duro,
e se c'è sicurezza
vendere mandorle a Kabul

16

With Haiku's Body:
I was gazed in mother's eyes
When I slipped from that piece of wood into the west Java waters!

با پیکر هایکو:

در دیده ی مادر دوخته شده بودم؛

وقتی در آب های غرب جاوا از تکه چوب جدا می شدم!

Con il corpo dell'Haiku:
Fissavo gli occhi di mia madre
mentre scivolavo
da quel pezzo di legno
nelle acque di Java

17

With Haiku's Body:
Most of them moved from Paktika,
They got cars and weapons along the way,
Now, they're in Behsood!

با پیکر هایکو:
خیلی شان از پکتیکا حرکت کردند،
موتر و تسلیحات در بین راه گرفتند،
حالا در بهسودند!

Con il corpo dell'Haiku:
Molti di loro
si sono trasferiti a Paktika,
hanno ottenuto automobili ed armi
lungo la via
ora si trovano a Behsood

18

With Haiku's Body:

(Taliban dialogue)

- Hazaras don't have a piece of land in all Afghanistan!

-hæ

How can they have land in Kandahar?

با پیکر هایکو:

– په ټول اوغانستان یو هزاره جایداد نلره!

هَ

په کندهار چټور لره؟

Con il corpo dell'Haiku:

(dialogo tra Talebani)

-gli Hazara non hanno un pezzo di terra in tutto l'Afghanistan!

-hæ! E come potrebbero avere delle terre a Kandahar?

19

With Haiku's Body:

A rainbow and geometrical shapes

The seventh night of Saratan was thrown a shadow for a while!

با پیکر هایکو:

رنگین کمان و چند فیگور هندسی

شب هفتم سرطان، تا پاسی سایه انداخته بود!

Con il corpo dell'Haiku:

Un arcobaleno

e figure geometriche

La settima notte di Saratan

per un attimo

un'ombra è stata gettata

20

With Haiku's Body:

Seems they sprayed a fist full of stars,

Nelson Mandela becomes a young man in Johannesburg!

با پیکر هایکو:

گویی یک مشت ستاره را پاشیده بودند،

نلسون ماندلا در ژوهانسبورگ جوان می شود!

Con il corpo dell'Haiku:

Sembra che abbiano gettato

un pugno di stelle nel cielo

Nelson Mandela

divenne un giovane uomo a Johannesburg

21

With Haiku's Body:
The pattern can be put everywhere,
It's even, I and you, man and woman

با پیکر هایکو:
نقش را می توان در همه جا گذاشت
حتایش را من، شما، او، هم زن و هم مرد

Con il corpo dell'Haiku:
Il modello potrebbe essere riproposto ovunque
Siamo anche io e te, uomo e donna

22

With Haiku's Body:
The eighth night of Saratan just goes forward by poetry,
It wasn't wearing its shoes when haiku came running!

با پیکر هایکو:

شب هشتم سرطان فقط با شعر پیش می رود

چپلی هایش را پایش نکرده بود که هایکو دوان دوان از راه رسید!

Con il corpo dell'Haiku:
L'ottava note di Saratan
va avanti solo grazie alla poesia
non indossava le scarpe
quando l'haiku arrivò correndo

23

With Haiku's Body

Does anyone have any news from Behsood and Daimirdad?

با پیکر هایکو:

جون 2013: از دایمیرداد و بهسود کسی خبری دارد؟

Con il corpo dell'Haiku:

Qualcuno ha qualche notizia da Behsood e Daimirdad?

24

With Haiku's Body:
Self-sinking is body and family abuse!

با پیکر هایکو:
خود غرق گردانی ظلم به بدن و خانواده است!

Con il corpo dell'Haiku:
L'auto-affondamento è abuso del corpo e della famiglia

25

With Haiku's Body:

In the heart of Kabul, there is a crossroads named Turabaz Khan. Turabaz Khan had a hand in torturing and killing of Abdul Khaliq Hazara, his family and his friends. I want to name this crossroads Abdul Khaliq Hazara. I ask all my friends to use this name. Abdul Khaliq Hazara crossroads!

با پیکر هایکو:

در دل کابل یک چهار راهی، چار راهی توره باز خان نام دارد. توره باز کسی ست که مستقیم در شکنجه و قتل شهید عبدالخالق هزاره و ده ها تن از یاران و اعضای خانواده اش دست داشت. من از این پس این چهار راهی را چهار راهی عبدالخالق هزاره می نامم. از دوستانم می خواهم شما هم همین نام را استفاده کنید. چهار راهی عبدالخالق هزاره!

Con il corpo dell'Haiku

Nel cuore di Kabul, c'è un incrocio chiamato Turabaz Khan.
Turabaz Khan contribuì a torturare e ad uccidere Abdul Khaliq Hazara,
la sua famiglia e i suoi amici. Io voglio rinominare questo incrocio
e chiamarlo Abdul Khaliq Hazara. Ho chiesto a tutti i miei amici
di utilizzare questo nome d'ora in poi. Incrocio Abdul Khaliq Hazara.

26

With Haiku's Body:

Sometimes some friends suggest thinking nationally. OK, nationally: why do the Kuchi Taliban abuse the rights not only of the Hazara, but of their own women and children?

با پیکر هایکو:

گاهی دوستانی پیشنهاد می کنند ملی بیاندیشیم. خب این هم ملی: چرا کوچی طالب نه تنها به هزاره بلکه به زن و کودک خود هم ظلم می کند؟

Con il corpo dell'Haiku:

A volte alcuni amici suggericono di pensare a livello nazionale.

Ok, nazionale: perché i Kuchi Talebani abusano dei diritti non solo degli Hazara

ma anche delle loro donne e bambini?

27

With Haiku's Body:

Let's think more nationally: Why don't our countrymen grow something other than poppy?

با پیکر هایکو:

بیاییم باز هم ملی تر فکر کنیم: چرا هموطنان ما زحمت نمی کشند چیز دیگری جز خشخاش کشت کنند؟

Con il corpo dell'Haiku:

Pensiamo in modo ancora più nazionale: perché i nostri connazionali non coltivano qualcosa di diverso dal papavero?

28

With Haiku's Body:

We imagine and some people make our imagination robots!

با پیکر هایکو:

ما تخیل می کنیم و تخیل های ما را عده ای ربات درست کرده اند

Con il corpo dell'Haiku:

Noi immaginiamo

e alcune persone

fanno della nostra immaginazione

un robot

29

With Haiku's Body:

When they returned from Behsood, they ripped Sushmita Banerjee's head skin

Then they shot her with twenty bullets

با پیکر هایکو:

وقتی از بهسود به پکتیکا برگشتند

پوست سر سوشمیتا بانرجی را کندند و بیست گلوله نثارش کردند

Con il corpo dell'Haiku:

Quando sono tornati da Behsud

hanno strappato la pelle

dalla testa di Sushmita Banerjee

poi le hanno sparato venti proiettili

30

With Haiku's Body:
- I came from Ashtarlay to Nili under moonlight!
Haiku was looking at me!

با پیکر هایکو:
- از اشترلی تا نیلی زیر نور ماه آمده ام!
هایکو نگاهم می کرد!

Con il corpo dell'Haiku:
Sono venuto da Ashtarlay a Nili
al chiaro di luna
un Haiku mi stava guardando

**Translation from English and Hazaragi to Italian:
Nicole Valentini and Basir Ahang**

Rodrigo Verdugo
Chile

(Santiago de Chile, 1977). Rodrigo began in the poetry workshop "Isla Negra" directed by the poet Edmund Herrera from 1922-1996 in La Sech. His work has been published in Chilean and international magazines and anthologies, and has been translated into English, French, Italian, Portuguese, Polish, Arabic, Uzbek, and Romanian.

In 2002 he published his first book *Nudos velados*, Ed Derrame. In 2005 he participated in the group exhibition "Derrame cono sur o el viaje de los argonautas"at the Fundación Eugenio Granell (Santiago de Compostela , Spain) and won first place in the "Alas de poesía" organized by the "Amigos de la poesía" (Monterrey, Mexico). In 2008 he participated with poets Rodrigo Hernandez and Marcela Albornoz Piceros Dachelet in editing the book " IDEM " by poet Armando Uribe, Coedición Ediciones Derrame, Editorial Universidad de Talca, and in the international exhibition of Surrealism "0 reverso do Olhar," in the House of Culture of Coimbra (Coimbra, Portugal).

In 2009 Rodrigo worked in the international exhibition of Surrealism "Iluminacoes Descontinuas" at the Convent of San José, (Lagoa, Portugal) and was invited to the XIX International Poetry Festival of Medellin (Medellin, Colombia). In 2011, he joined in the Collective exhibition "El inverso del universo," a tribute to the centenary of Roberto Matta, organized by the Foundation Itau. In 2012 he participated in the Collective exhibition "Surrealims 2012" at the Googleworks Center for the Arts (Pennsylvania, USA).

Rodrigo is working on a second book, *Anuncio*, (to be published by Ediciones AC) and on other unpublished books: *Ventanas Quebradas* and *Transmision debajo de las piedras*. He is also the Director of Taller literario "Joan Brossa," del Centre Catala.

HAZARA, WE WILL SPEAK YOUR LANGUAGE

Hazara, we will speak your language

There will be a waking in the desert

Strangers will leave a crown of auras.

Until the dawn we will stand

No rush on the roots.

We'll watch your key with bone weapons

The day has the sound of an animal who drinks water

Hemispheric Trizadura

Echo within the voice

I hear the animal drinking water

No rush on the roots.

We will speak your language

We will dream that your key embodies

An animal drinking water

The power of the night make him load fundamental ashes.

HAZARA HABLAREMOS TU LENGUA

Hazara, hablaremos tu lengua

Habrá vigilia en el desierto

Una corona de auras dejaran los extraños.

Hasta el alba estaremos de pie

No hay prisa en las raíces.

Vigilaremos tu clave con armas de hueso

El dia tiene el sonido de un animal que bebe agua

Trizadura hemisferica

Eco dentro de la voz

Escucho al animal beber agua

No hay prisa en las raíces.

Hablaremos tu lengua

Soñaremos que tu clave encarna

Un animal esta bebiendo agua

El poderío de la noche le hace cargar fundamentos de ceniza.

Mildred Kiconco Barya
Uganda

Mildred Kiconco Barya is a Ugandan author of three poetry collections: *Give Me Room to Move My Feet, The Price of Memory after the Tsunami,* and *Men Love Chocolates But They Don't Say.* She has also published short stories in various anthologies, and taught creative writing at the Alabama School of Fine Arts in Birmingham (USA).

Mildred is a board member of the African Writers Trust, and currently a PhD fellow at the University of Denver, Colorado. She blogs at: http://mildredbarya.com/.

HERE AND NOW: HAZARA

If anyone tells you
This is not your country
Your land, your mountains, your home
Do not believe them.

For centuries you've fought and fled
Hunted and haunted like game
Let it be your choice to
Stand. Or sit it out

You belong as much as your enemies
Claim this place. This space that marks you
Unwanted.
I see your reflection in my mirror
In my freedom dreams
You're me. I am you,
Together
Us.

Stefaan van den Bremt
Flanders, Belgium

Stefaan is a poet and the honorary chairman of PEN FLANDERS.

Get rid of that calendar full of tear-off wisdom.
That day will not go away.

Once in a blue moon someone pulled up a chair.
For a short spell an unknown guest came.

He couldn't stay, but sat at the table,
ladled a plate full of shadow, filled a glass

with light, slurped it up and left;
he could not stay where he was.

Since then that guest resides in you.
One day he came for a whole day.

Even now you don't know what to do with yourself
And sit at table with the chair on which he sat.

Arroja ese calendario lleno de saberes desechables.
Aquel día no quiere pasar.

Aquel día alguien acercó una silla.
Un lunes cualquiera, un huésped extraño vino.

No podía quedarse, pero se sentó a la mesa,
colmó un plato de sombra, llenó un vaso

de luz, lo sorbió, y se fue;
no pudo quedarse donde estaba.

Desde ese día aquel huésped te habita.
Una vez vino una noche y un día.

Aún hoy no sabes qué hacer contigo
en la mesa frente a la silla en la que él se sentó.

Winston Morales Chavarro
Colombia

Neiva, Huila, 1969. Comunicador Social y Periodista. Magíster en Estudios de la Cultura, mención Literatura Hispanoamericana, Universidad Andina Simón Bolívar de Quito. Profesor de tiempo completo en la Universidad de Cartagena, Colombia. Ha ganado los concursos de poesía Organización Casa de Poesía, 1996; José Eustasio Rivera, 1997 y 1999; Concursos Departamentales del Ministerio de Cultura, 1998; Euclides Jaramillo Arango, Universidad del Quindío, 2000; Segundo premio Concurso Nacional de Poesía

Ciudad de Chiquinquirá, 2000; Concurso Nacional de Poesía Universidad de Antioquia, 2001; Tercer Lugar en el Concurso Internacional Literario de Outono, Brasil. Primer Premio IX Bienal Nacional de Novela José Eustasio Rivera. Primer Puesto en el Premio Nacional de Poesía Universidad Tecnológica de Bolívar, Cartagena, 2005. Ganador de una residencia artística del Grupo de los tres del Ministerio de Cultura, Colombia, y el Foncas, de México, con su proyecto: "Paralelos de lo invisible: Chichén Itza-San Agustín". Primer puesto Concurso de Cuento Humberto Tafur Charry, 2013. Finalista en varios concursos de poesía y cuento en Colombia, España, Argentina y México.

Ha publicado los libros de poemas *Aniquirona*, Trilce Editores, 1998; *La lluvia y el ángel* (Coautoría)-Trilce Editores, 1999; *De regreso a Schuaima*, Ediciones Dauro, Granada-España, 2001; *Memorias de Alexander de Brucco*, Editorial Universidad de Antioquia, 2002; *Summa poética*, Altazor Editores, 2005; *Antología, Colección Viernes de Poesía, Universidad Nacional,* 2009; *Camino a Rogitama,* Trilce Editores, 2010; *La Ciudad de las piedras que cantan*, Caza de Libros, Ibagué 2011, y Temps era temps, Altazor Editores, Bogotá, 2013.

En narrativa: *Dios puso una sonrisa sobre su rostro*, novela, 2004; en ensayo: *Poéticas del ocultismo en las escrituras de José Antonio Ramos Sucre, Carlos Obregón, César Dávila Andrade y Jaime Sáenz*, Trilce Editores, Bogotá, 2008. Poemas suyos han aparecido en revistas y periódicos de Colombia, España, Venezuela, Italia, Estados Unidos, Argentina, Puerto Rico y México, y han sido traducidos al francés, italiano, portugués e inglés.

HAZARA

I breathe

I hold the breaths between one life and another
It is all that is left
What I encapsulate on the road to death

It all happens so fast,
We hardly raise our sight toward the air
And another dart is shot
With the currishness that shots the atribute
The dream
The hugsty place they set each time a writer dies.

Between one life and another
There will be always a breath to be picked up
A lament to collect.

The rope that was thrown since chilhood
Goes on crumbling until it is only that:
Another breath;

It is as if one picked up with nostalgia
the luggage that has been dropped by the roadside.

No one knows who are their owners
Or what it has within

Between luggage and candles
Life goes on crumbling
What is left of its breath

The breath could be our own:
A shy hope packed by fate for those still to die.

English translation: Luis Rafael Gálvez

HAZARA

Respiro

Me tomo los alientos que hay entre una vida y otra.

Es lo único que queda

Lo que logro encapsular en el camino por la muerte.

Todo sucede tan a prisa,

Apenas levanta uno la vista al aire

Y otro dardo es disparado

Con la mezquindad que se dispara el atributo

El sueño,

La pocilga que se tiende cada vez que fallece un escritor.

Entre una vida y otra

Siempre habrá un resuello por recoger

Un lamento por coleccionar.

El cáñamo que se arrojó desde la infancia

Se va desmenuzando hasta quedar reducido a eso:

Otro aliento;

Es como si uno recogiera con nostalgia

Los fardos que van tirando a la vera del camino.

Nadie sabe quiénes son sus dueños

Nadie lo que llevan dentro.

Entre fardo y velas

Se va desmoronando la vida,

Lo que queda de su vaho.

El aliento puede ser el nuestro:

Una tímida esperanza empaquetada para la suerte de los que faltan por morir.

Esteban Valdés Arzate
Mexico

Esteban Valdés Arzate was born in Mexico City in 1947. He was raised in México and New York, and actually lives in Puerto Rico. He studied science and history at the University of Puerto Rico where he earned an M.A. In the 70s he founded the magazine *Alicia la Roja* (*Red Alice*). In 1977 he published *Fuera de Trabajo*, Puerto Rico's first concrete poetry book. In the 80s he worked with *La Mueca*, a clandestine satirical newspaper, and with the *Editorial La Iguana Dorado*, organized the National Encounter of Poets.
Estaban has participated in multiple exhibitions at galleries and museums. An anarcho-syndicalist, in 1984, he founded the Labor Department Brotherhood (HEDET) as the organization secretary and later President. He became the principal delegate to the General Union of Workers.

STAR SONNET

* * * * * * * * * *
* * * * * * * * * *
* * * * * * * * * *
* * * * * * * * * *

* * * * * * * * * *
* * * * * * * * * *
* * * * * * * * * *
* * * * * * * * * *

* * * * * * * * * *
* * * * * * * * * *
* * * * * * * * * *

* * * * * * * * * *
* * * * * * * * * *
* * * * * * * * * *

Akwasi Aidoo
Ghana/USA

Akwasi Aidoo is the founding Executive Director of TrustAfrica, a foundation dedicated to advancing democratic governance and equitable development in Africa. He is the Chair of the Boards of the Fund for Global Human Rights, the Open Society Initiative for West Africa, and Resource Alliance.

Akwasi has taught at universities in Ghana, Tanzania, and the United States. He was educated in Ghana and the United States, and received a PhD in medical sociology from the University of Connecticut in 1985. He writes poetry and fiction every day.

THIS-CRIME-NATION

We move in clear voice together
With verse metered to the heights of Hazara
Pain and lodge this PoemPlate loads of
Justice against batterers of your dreams and

We move on this-crime-nation to account
On account of stretches countless in cutovers
Marked by limbs of Hazara dignity kidnaped and
Massacred timeless in fashion steady

In lands *-istan* and *-an* where faith, peace-named,
Calls but denied for dogma traded & maimed
They try & try… maiming dry and you cry… but
We cheer your rising spirit on the endless lands you share

We salute with hands clasped the wise
Ways in your dignity & spirit even when your smile
Is robbed in full view of our naked eyes & ditched a mile
Deep beneath their troughs of dis-crimi-nation & pillage

They condemn you, the irrepressible kite runner, but
We, the PoemTeam, sprint across oceans
"For you, a thousand times over" and declare:
Beyond this-crime-nation, the Hazara shall rise again!

Yolanda Pantin
Venezuela

Yolanda Pantin was born in Caracas, Venezuela, in 1954. She studied Literature at the Universidad Católica Andrés Bello in Caracas. She is the author of *Casa o Lobo* (1981), *Correo del Corazón* (1985), *La Canción Fría* (1989), *Poemas del Escritor* (1989), *El Cielo de París* (1989), *Los Bajos Sentimientos* (1993), *La Quietud* (1998), *El Hueso Pélvico* (2002), *Poemas Huérfanos* (2002), *La Épica del Padre* (2002), *País* (2007), *21 Caballos* (2011).

Yolanda has published three anthologies, two of them in Spain and the other in México. In 2004 she published her complete works in Caracas and is preparing a new 2013 edition in Spain.

Several of her poems have been translated into English, Dutch, German, Korean, Chinese, Portuguese, and Italian and been published in scholarly journals and anthologies of contemporary poetry. She has published several children's books.

Her play *La Otredad y el Vampiro* was translated into German, and was included in an anthology of contemporary Latin American women playwrights.

Yolanda has been invited to participate in numerous poetry and literary conferences in Mexico, Guatemala, Colombia, Peru, Argentina, Uruguay, France, Spain, Holland, Italy, Portugal, Germany, Israel, the USA, Dominican Republic, Nicaragua, and El Salvador.

In 1989 she was awarded the Fundarte Poetry Prize in Caracas. She was a fellow of the Rockefeller Foundation Bellagio Study Center. In 2004 she received a Guggenheim Fellowship.

BAMIYAN

I was close, facing the clouds
but I could imagine and I still can
through your difficult paths
finding the way to the place
where Buddha first
had a human face.
Who was going to tell you, people
of Hazara, that this alley
would arrive at its share of madness,
ministry of promotion
of virtue and prevention
of vice?
They destroyed the colossal
incarnations of the Buddha,
but to obliterate you
it is not possible.

BAMIYÁN

Estuve cerca, de cara a las nubes
pero podía imaginarte y todavía puedo
a través de tus difíciles caminos
encontrar el paso hasta el lugar
donde Buda por primera vez
tuvo rostro humano.

¿Quién les iba a decir, gente
de Hazara, que este callejón
llegaría en su parte de locura,
a un ministerio de promoción
de la virtud y prevención
del vicio?

Destruyeron las colosales
encarnaciones del Buda,
pero borrarlos a ustedes
no es posible.

Yiorgos Chouliaras
Greece

Yiorgos Chouliaras is a Greek poet and essayist, whose poems in English translation have been published and reviewed in major literary periodicals, including *Agenda, Grand Street, Harvard Review, Poetry, Ploughshares, The Iowa Review*, and *World Literature Today*. His work also appeard in the anthology, *New European Poets*.

Yiorgos' work has also been translated into Croatian, French, Spanish, Turkish, and other languages. He is the author of six volumes of poetry in Greek and of numerous essays on literature and cultural history, in English as well as Greek. He has translated works of several poets, including Wallace Stevens.

Yiorgos was a co-founder of the influential Greek literary reviews, *Tram* and *Hartis*, and has edited literary and scholarly publications in the United States. He has served on the Board of the Hellenic Authors' Society, the Poets Circle, the Ottawa International Writers Festival, and the Modern Greek Studies Association.

Educated at Reed College and at The Graduate Faculty of the New School for Social Research, Yiorgos lived and worked in Oregon, New York City, Ottawa, Boston, Washington, D.C., and Dublin, before returning to Athens. His forthcoming *Dictionary of Memories* is a "memoir" in the form of a dictionary.

HAZARA

If it is a hazard to be human,

then we all are Hazara,

as it will still be true even when

                     it will no longer be a hazard

REFUGEES

On the other side
of the photograph I write to remind myself
not where and when but who

I am not in the photograph

They left us nothing
to take with us
Only this photograph

If you turn it over you will see me

Is that you in the photograph, they ask me
I don't know what to tell you

Translated by David Mason & the author

Γιώργος Χουλιάρας
ΠΡΟΣΦΥΓΕΣ

Από την άλλη πλευρά
της φωτογραφίας γράφω για να θυμάμαι
όχι το πού και πότε αλλά ποιος

Δεν είμαι εγώ στη φωτογραφία
Τίποτε δεν μας άφησαν
να πάρουμε μαζί μας
Μόνον αυτή τη φωτογραφία

Αν τη γυρίσετε από την άλλη θα με δείτε

Εσύ είσαι στη φωτογραφία, με ρωτούν
Δεν ξέρω τι να σας πω

James O'Hara
New Mexico, USA and County Kerry, Ireland

James O'Hara, who is from County Kerry Ireland and lives in Santa Fe New Mexico, believes the responsibility of the poet is to hold within his arms the moral boundaries of his people.

CRASH THE SUN

Do you wish to live forever
Your beliefs invite our feet to earth
to satisfy our appetites for energy and for flesh

We will fill your eyes with boiling blood
and tourniquet the healthy limbs of your men

Then you will plead and hold the babies close to you
while we tear up the soil and savour your despair

We lay waste the innocence
and ruin the brightness in your daughters

Crash the sun
hands and knees of elders in the burning roadways

In rags of skin
you will ask for water

and we will dye the mountains red as if of wool
until we bring your place to silence

Raquel Chalfi
Israel

Raquel Chalfi was born in Tel-Aviv, Israel, where she lives and works. She has (so far) published fifteen books of poetry and one of prose.

Raquel is the recipient of several literary awards, which include the Bialik Poetry Award and the Brenner Poetry Award. She is also an Independent filmmaker and a playwright.

PRECIPICE

I sit on the other side
of the globe, finally finding the fraction
of time, finally grasping a fleeting
gasp of determination
to look, to probe, to try to touch
the predicament of the Hazara people.
The pictures. The pictures delicately
sing, weep: Look!
Children, old men, men, women
human beings living, trying to hold onto
life at the very edge of the Precipice - - -
My D.N.A., my own people's D.N.A.,
(Hebrew, ancient, Jewish)
know it, know it all too intimately - - -
How can my few, feeble, utterances
make a change?
The sweeping force the wind of
history, of politics –
flows through us all.
How can it be touched by the miniscule, tiny twitch
of a butterfly's wing of a
prayer?
 How, how to make
a tiny difference

for the sake of one
Hazara child?

Jim Byron
USA

Dylan's back, but this time he's Jameson, aka Jim Byron, who sounds like Youth Spirit incarnate (akin not only to Bob but also Conor Oberst and Daniel Johnston). A kindly soul, likely candidate for the spokesperson for his generation, maniac of invention, generating songs or poems during any good week, his lyrics manage brilliance and innocence with a poignant voice sure to mess with your heart.

LIBERTY, COME GALLOPING! SALVATION, FLOWER!

For the Hazara of Afghanistan & Pakistan

Because the chosen people were always the unrepresented,
And, driven hither and thither, across a perilous, destitute planet,
They remained diligent, resolved, peaceful, true and strong;
Though no man can know whom divinity has set aside,
Still I must support the Hazara, who traversed across deserts,

And multitudinous skies, who fled from oppression, or who
Raised arms against monstrous enemies of life, liberty and truth.
I must support the Hazara, who inhabited homes carved in stone,
Who weathered the putrid dust of the Afghan-Pakistani desert, bravely.
Courageous regardless of whatever route necessitated,

For the Hazara, the persecuted of the persecuted in a battle
Against fear itself, must breathe courage to survive. I must
Support the Hazara wholeheartedly for the sheer audacity,
The sheer humanity- the dignity, the hope, the very inner
Light of my conscience commands- for daring to read

The signs written in the stars, in books, the hearts, minds,
And in the very soul of Truth itself. For the Hazara, the
Desert-bound, the meek, the righteous, the jailed and exiled,
Destiny, abide. And Fate, step aside. For the Hazara,
Liberty, come galloping! Galloping, I say! Salvation, flower unto Hazaristan.

Luisa Vicioso Sánchez
Dominican Republic

Luisa Vicioso Sánchez, 52, from the Dominican Republic, currently serves as an Ambassador for Women, Children, and Adolescent issues at the Ministry of Foreign Affairs. She has also worked as a National Program Officer for UNICEF, dealing with issues relating to women and education. Her previous roles have included consultancies with UNIFEM and UNESCO.

HAITI (HAZARA)

I imagine you a virgin land
before precursors pirates
took off your mahogany clothes
and left you thus
with your round breasts uncovered
and your grass skirt torn
barely green
brown, shy.

Haiti (Hazara)
I imagine you as a teen
scented with vetiver
tender with dew
without that multitude of scars
they'll integrate you with in the market of maps
and offer multicolor you up
on the sidewalks of Port Prince
in Jacmel, in San Marcos, in the Artibonite
as a big tinplate bargain.

Haiti (Hazara)
eager hiker you____ smile to me
interrupting sidewalk siestas
crushing stones
paving dust

Luisa Vicioso Sánchez

with your bare sweaty feet.

Haiti (Hazara)
crafter of art in a thousand ways
you paint the stars with your hands
for you I understood
that love and hate
as you are called.

Note: here is my poem, because for me all struggling people are name Haiti, the native name of my island.

HAITI (HAZARA)

Te imagino virgen
antes de que piratas precursores
te quitaran tus vestidos de caoba
y te dejaran asi
con tu senos redondos al aire
y tu falda de hierba desgarrada
apenas verde
marron timida.

Haiti (Hazara)
te imagino adolescente
olorosa a vetiver
tierna de rocio
sin esa multitud de cicatrices
con que te integraron al mercado de mapas
y con que te ofrecen multicolor
en las aceras de puerto principe
en jacmel, en san marcos, en el artibonite
en un gran baratillo de hojalata.

Haiti (Hazara)
caminante que afanosa me sonries
interrumpiendo siestas de veredas
aplastando piedras

asfaltando polvo

con tus pies sudorosos y descalzos.

Haiti (Hazara)

que tejes el arte de mil formas

y que pintas las estrellas con tus manos

por ti entendi

que el amor y el odio

como tu se llaman.

Andrea Garbin
Italy

Andrea Garbin lives and works in the province of Mantova (Italy). He has published the poetry books, *Il sensodella musa*, *Lattice*, *Viaggio di un guerriero senz'arme*, and *Croce del sud* He has also published short stories and anthologies, and writes for the theatre.

Andrea directs the literary meetings at the Coffee Bar Galeter in Montichiari (BS) with the participation of many local poets and artists. He also collaborates with Beppe Costa and "Casa della poesia (House of Poetry)" in Baronissi, especially with Jack Hirschman and Paul Polansky.

In Rome Andrea meets with Fernando Arrabal, for whom he translated into the dialect of Mantova, the poems "Ma fellatrice idolâtrée" and "Clitoris."

On June 19, 2010 he created the *Manifesto Letterario dal Sottosuolo (Manifesto from the Literary Underground)* signed by a dozen authors. For the theater, he collaborated with the Living Theatre and the Odin Teatret and he was the founder of the "Teatro Scariolante."

Probably i know that a bomb can:
in every instant to explode,
be shattered, to shatter the earth,
be sticked in the flesh, to infect,
simply to eat the life,
to disfigure, to break the knees
of a child in run, to make a collapse,
to transform the lips into a silence,
the eyes in tears and the ears
in a continuous terror, to blossom,
to bloom under the feet of a village,
to break the bones, to dry up the neck.
Probably i know everything this
but i've never seen it, ever felt,
ever touch neither lived, never.
The apocalypse you have it to you every day,
you are not the first ones and you won't be the last,
it is to us, to all of us, now, to make it stop,
to break the tongue of the indifferent snake.

Probabilmente io so che una bomba può:
in ogni istante deflagrare,
frantumarsi, frantumare la terra,
conficcarsi nella carne, infettare,
semplicemente mangiarsi la vita,
sfigurare, le ginocchia spezzare
di un bambino in corsa, far crollare,
trasformare le labbra in un silenzio,
gli occhi in lacrime e le orecchie
in un continuo terrore, sbocciare,
fiorire sotto i piedi di un villaggio,
le ossa spezzare, il collo prosciugare.
Probabilmente io so tutto questo
ma non l'ho mai visto, mai sentito,
mai tastato né vissuto, mai.
L'apocalisse voi l'avete tutti i giorni,
non siete i primi e non sarete gli ultimi,
sta a noi, a noi tutti, ora, farlo smettere,
spezzare la lingua del serpente indifferente.

Luz Helena Cordero Villamizar
Colombia

Luz Helena Cordero Villamizar was born in Bucaramanga, Colombia, and is a professional psychologist with an MA in Literature. She has written short stories, poems and essays. Luz has been included in all recent anthologies of Colombian poetry and has been awarded several prizes.

Poetry
Postal de la memoria (*Postal of Memory*), Caza de libros, Ibagué, 2010
Por arte de palabras (*By Art of Words*). Bogotá: Universidad Externado de Colombia, 2009.

Cielo ausente (Absent Heaven), Ediciones Sociedad de la Imaginación, Bogotá, 2001
Óyeme con los ojos, (*Hear Me with Your Eyes*) Trilce Editores, Bogotá, 1996

Short fiction
Canción para matar el miedo, Editorial Magisterio, Bogotá, 1997
El puente está quebrado, Editorial Magisterio, Bogotá, 1998

VERSES LIKE PATHS

I have to write a poem to the Hazara

I don't know where they are

I don't know its people

I´ve seen their faces on the network

cute and deep children's eyes

hurried women

agitated men seeking exits

but the exits are beyond their rough hands

that are useful to caress the soil.

Something unnameable,

something that I want to move away from the poem

that obstructs the doors, closes the roads, detonates the dreams

and the colours of the detonation can't be painted by children

I know nothing about the Hazara

but they are generous like a freshly baked bread

I know they have my eyes and my skin

and their fear scrabbles my certainties and my faith

I know my voice is so useless

like that flower that emerges on a desolated road

only with the hope somebody will see it

Instead of verses, I would like to send roads

paths and flowers to the Hazara people.

VERSOS COMO CAMINOS

He de escribir un poema para el pueblo Hazara

No sé dónde hallarlo

No conozco su gente

He visto sus rostros en la red

bellos y profundos ojos de niños

mujeres que se afanan

hombres agitados que buscan salidas

pero las salidas no están en sus manos rudas

que les sirven para acariciar la tierra.

Algo innombrable, algo que quiero alejar del poema

obstruye las puertas, cierra los caminos, estalla los sueños

y los colores de esa detonación no pueden ser pintados por los niños.

No sé nada sobre los hazaras

pero son nobles como un pan recién horneado

Sé que tienen mis ojos y mi piel

y su miedo escarba mis certezas y mi fe.

Sé que mi voz es tan inútil

como esa flor que brota en un camino desolado

sólo por la esperanza de que alguien la vea.

En lugar de versos, quisiera enviar caminos,

caminos y flores para los hazaras.

Peter Voelker
Germany

Peter Voelker (61) was born in Gruendau-Rothenbergen (Germany). After qualifying as a Certified Forwarding Agent he worked in all branches of the Transport Industry. Working in Hamburg as a Certified Shipping Agent, he switched to the German Transport Publishing House in the early eighties. He wrote and edited there for two years as the Responsible Editor in the Foreign Trade Department.

During this time he was in contact with the Hamburg workshop of the "Werkkreis Literatur Arbeitswelt" (Literature Workshop of the Working World). From 1982 to 1989 he was the Managing Editor for European Politics in the United Economic Service (VWD) news service in Eschborn, Germany.

Towards the end of the eighties he became co-editor of the alternative magazine *Neue Hanauer Zeitung* (*NHZ*). Together with political friends he established the "Solidaritaetsfonds demokratischer Medien in der Welt e.V., Goeppingen" in 1993. This organization supports independent media and art projects throughout the world. He is currently a member of the directorate. From November 1989 to March 2007 Peter was the General Secretary of the Media and Film Department of the German Media Trade Union in Stuttgart and Berlin. In this capacity he wrote several articles for books on the future of the media.

Today Peter is one of the artists of the "Kulturstation Kaufmann" in Gelnhausen, Germany. He has published thirteen books of lyric poetry. In the 2014 he received the top poetry award for his book *Agamemnon and Kassandra* in Lakonia from the International Academy of Arts "Orient – Ocident" (Romania).

NEW SIGHTS

Hungry for new sights,
I wandered beneath
summer green beeches
with friends,
treading with more
than wonted care,
I saw the eternal light
stream through the leaves,
saw too the flies
drinking the early rays,
spiders weaving lacework
in the dewfall,
heard ants screech
and the moss moan,
saw worms gobbling
their way into the dark,
sensed bacterial vapours,
life rotting slow
between grass
stalks and wispy heads,
saw, as day passed
and night approached,
we humans are like they
- of stardust born.

Peter Voelker

ON ART AND LOVE

Art and love

are not found

in seeking.

They find you,

down by the river and

deep within.

There's no profit made

from art and love.

They cannot be sold.

Turn your back on

art and love,

and watch something wonderful slip away -

the oneness with the water as it flows,

the intimacy of a loved one.

Art and love go on forever.

There can be no death with love.

Translated and edited by: Lucy James

ÜBER DIE KUNST UND DIE LIEBE

Die Kunst und die Liebe
wirst du nicht finden,
solange du sie suchst.
Sie müssen dir begegnen,
draußen am Fluss und
in deinem tiefsten Inneren.
Aus der Kunst und der Liebe
kannst du keinen Gewinn machen.
Sie sind unverkäuflich.
Du kannst etwas Wunderbares versäumen,
wenn du sie nicht zulässt,
die Kunst und die Liebe,
die Einheit mit dem dahinfließenden Wasser,
die Nähe zu einem geliebten Menschen.
Kunst und Liebe sind unvergänglich.
Nichts ist vergänglich, was geliebt wird.

NEUER BLICK

Auf einen neuen Blick,
gemeinsam mit Freunden,
ließ ich mich ein unter
sommergrünen Buchen,
setzte die Schritte
achtsamer als sonst,
sah das ewige Licht
in die Blätter strömen,
sah auch die Läuse
das frühe Licht trinken,
Spinnen Kunstnetze weben,
in der Morgenfeuchte,
hörte Ameisen schreien
und das Moos stöhnen,
sah Würmer, sich in
die Finsternis fressen,
ahnte Bakterienschäume,
das Leben verwesen
zwischen den Halmen
und Rispen der Gräser,
begriff zwischen Tag
und kommender Nacht,
wir Menschen sind wie sie,
aus Sternenstaub gemacht.

Zoran Anchevski
Macedonia

Zoran Anchevski (b.1954) graduated with a degree in English Language and Literature from the Faculty of Philology at Skopje University, where he currently teaches British and American literature. He received his M.A. in American literature from California State University, and a PhD in comparative literature from Skopje University.

He has published the following books of poetry: *Journey through Broken Images* (1984), *Strategy of Defeat* (1994), *Line(s) of High Resistance* (1998), *Translating the Dead* (2000), *Wild Peace* (2004), *Selected Poems* (2008), *History of the Wind* (2009), *Selected Poems* (in English, 2011), and *Celestial Pantomime* (forthcoming). They have all been well received by critics and highly acclaimed and have earned various awards including the international Giacomo Leopardi Award (2004) in Italy.

Zoran has also published several essays, reviews, and a book-length study in literary theory and criticism, titled *Of Tradition* (2008). He is the editor and translator of several poetry anthologies in English and an anthology of contemporary short stories (*Change of the System*, 2000). He also translated many literary works by such authors as: W. B. Yeats, T.S. Eliot, W.H. Auden, Ted Hughes, Seamus Heaney, Derek Walcott, Yehuda Amichai, John Ashbery, W.S. Merwin, Kenzaburo Oe, Toni Morison, Makoto Ooka, etc.

Selections from his poetry have been translated into Albanian, Bulgarian, Chinese, English, French, Finnish, Galician, German, Greek, Hebrew, Italian, Portuguese, Romanian, Russian, Serbo-Croat, Slovenian, Spanish, Turkish, Ukrainian, and been published in various magazines and anthologies at home and abroad.

Zoran is a member of the Macedonian Writers' Union, the Literary Federation for World Peace (member of the International Advisory Board), was two times the secretary of Macedonian P.E.N., and the former president of the Organizing Board of the renowned Struga International Poetry Festival (2002-2007).

EMIGRANTS' POEM

Isn't this skin enough for us

that we naturally according to need

ourselves cast,

then trudge like tramps

wander the world

infected with *polyglossia*

struck dumb by the Babylonian virus—

a circus!

We forget the taste

of our mother's milk

and the labour pains

of our first words.

And what if we know for sure

the head of the delta

when the flow is everything:

spring, confluence, consolation,

excitement and diving

into the fleeting essence—

a nonsense!

Faceless

we search for the footprints,

echoes of our laughter and our poverty,

Zoran Anchevski

our weeping and our wealth,

day in day out dig ditches—

graves

that time fills up

planting them with sharp spears

to prevent our return.

**Translated into English by the author,
Graham and Peggy W. Reid**

Naotaka Uematsu
Japan

WAR AND CHILDREN
戦争の子供たち

Children are playing on the street under the bullets.

Children never be scared of the sound of air raid.

Children are laughing under the wars.

「銃弾の飛び交う街で子等遊ぶ」
「子供等は爆撃音におびえない」
「子供等は戦争の狭間で笑ってる」。

奈良市北登美が丘4－15－8

TANKA DEDICATED TO THE HAZARA

Walk Hazara, Walk straight like a rhinoceros, through the beautiful fields of Bamiyan.

Gods love Bamiyan, love those limpid eyes of countryfolks.

ハザラの人々への短歌

「犀の如くまっすぐ歩めハザラ人
　その麗しきバーミアンの野を」

「神々は愛したまえりバーミアン、その里人の澄んだ瞳を」

Paul Disnard
Colombia

Colombiano, reside indistintamente en Serbia y en Colombia. Licenciado en Etnologia de la Universidad de Belgrado. En su último libro EN LA OTRA ORILLA DEL VIENTO incluye todos sus pequeños libros de cuentos y poemas publicados con anterioridad. Ha sido Cónsul de Colombia en Yugoslavia, dirigió la biblioteca de la Embajada de México en Belgrado y siendo estudiante hizo parte del equipo de lenguas extranjeras de Radio Yugoslavia, emisiones en español.

HAZARA

I am an enemy of the birds in cages,

an enemy of the chains that humiliate dogs

an enemy of those who do not respect the life of animals

who have been born free in the woods, in swamps,

in the highest mountains where eagles

write in heaven their love for the land

I exalt my love for Hazara women,

for Hazara men, for their children who tomorrow

will also be free men

and I raise my fist against the oppressors,

against despots,

because those same chains make the gallows

that will kill the devil emirs

and there won't be a single poet in the world who does not remember

Gandhi's resistance, toughness, strength

the apostle, the combatant,

the angel of victory

a burning torch against the wind!

Raise your fists, Hazara,

gather the stones and slings for David

to overthrow Goliath again

Hail, Hazara!,

you are one more

Paul Disnard

with us

to raise a new world without tyrants!

HAZARA

Soy enemigo de los pájaros en jaulas,
enemigo de las cadenas que humillan a los perros,
enemigo de quienes no respetan la vida de los animales
que han nacido libres en los bosques, en los pantanos,
en las montañas más altas donde las águilas
escriben en el cielo su amor por la tierra,
exalto mi amor por las mujeres Hazara,
por los hombres Hazara, por los niños que mañana
tambien serán hombres libres
y levanto mi puño contra los opresores,
contra los despotas,
porque esas mismas cadenas harán las horcas
que acabarán con los emires del diablo
y no habrá un solo poeta en el mundo que recuerde
la resistencia, la tenacidad, la forfaleza de Ghandi
el apóstol, el combatiente
el angel de la victoria.

Levantad los pùños, Hazara,
recoged las piedras y las hondas para que David
una vez más dé con Goliat en tierra-

!Salve, Hazara!,
eres uno más

con nosotros

para levantar un mundo nuevo sin tiranos!

Jamundi - Colombia, marzo 29 del 2013

Vyacheslav Kupriyanov
Russia

Poet, Translator and Critic Vyacheslav Kupriyanov was born in Novosibirsk, Russia in 1939. Kupriyanov is a member of the Russian Writers Union, Serbian Writers Union and Russian PEN. In 2010, he won Bunin Prize for his literary works.

APPEL

yellow

black

white

this blood

of all of as

is just

as red

stop

the tests

LLAMAMIENTO

Los amarillos

los negros

los blancos

la sangre nuestra

es igualmente

roja

basta de

averiguar.

Gabriel Rosenstock
Ireland

Gabriel Rosenstock is a poet, novelist, playwright, author, and translator of over 170 books, mostly in Irish. He was taught the art of haiku at the Schule für Dichtung (Poetry Academy) in Vienna and the Hyderabad Literary Festival, India. Gabriel also writes for children.

Among the anthologies in which he is represented are *Best European Fiction 2012* (Dalkey Archive Press), and *Haiku in English: The First Hundred Years* (W. W. Norton & Co. 2013). *Books Ireland*, Summer 2012, says of his comic novel *My Head is Missing:* 'This is a departure for Rosenstock but he is surefooted as he takes on the comic genre and writes a story full of engaging characters and a plot that keeps the reader turning the page.'

Where Light Begins is a selection of haiku and *The Invisible Light* features haiku in Irish, English, Spanish, and Japanese with work by American master photographer Ron Rosenstock. His latest book is a bilingual volume of poems, *Sasquatch* (Arlen House 2013).

SQUID: PHOTO OF AN EMBRYO

five day old embryo.

you look to be whole

but you are not yet of this world.

you appear to be staring at me

as though about to say something

not on your own behalf

but on behalf of all embryos:

a secret never to be shared with me.

I see you as colour, a thing, a shape

that's all. what do you see?

was there a flash from the camera that startled you

terrorised you?

do you know what pain is? pleasure?

can you hear anything? a squeak?

three hearts you possess. three hearts. how can you bear it?

embryo five days old.

I feel you are much older than me

and that you and your kind will be around

you and your ink/ in the flowing sea

when we've been swept from the planet

the one-hearted species.

Poem in Irish (Gaelic) and prose translation by Gabriel Rosenstock

MÁTHAIR SHÚIGH: GRIANGHRAF DE GHIN

Gin cúig lá d'aois.

Féachann tú iomlán

Ach níl tú tagtha fós ar an saol.

An chuma ort gur ag stánadh orm atá tú

Is tú ar tí rud éigin a rá

Ní ar do shon féin ach ar son gach sutha:

Rún nach roinnfear liom go brách.

Mar dhath, mar mheall, mar chruth a fheicimse thú.

Sin uile. Cad is léir duitse?

An raibh scal ón gceamara ann a bhain preab asat,
A chuir sceimhle ionat?

An eol duit cad is pian ann? Pléisiúr?

Gabriel Rosenstock

An gcloiseann tú aon ní?

Rud ar bith? Gíocs?

Trí chroí atá ionat. Trí chroí. Conas a sheasann tú é!

Gin cúig lá d'aois.

Braithim gur sine i bhfad thú ná mé

Is go mbeidh tusa is do leithéid fós thart

Tú féin is do dhúch

Sa tsrúill

Is sinne glanta go deo den phláinéad,

Speiceas aonchroíoch.

Maruja Vieira
Colombia

Vieira Maruja was born in Manizales, Colombia on December 25, 1922. She is a poet and professor of Language at the Spanish Royal Academy. Her poetry has been translated into English, French, German, Greek, Hungarian and Galician.

Poetry Books:
Bell Of Rain Bogotá, 1947
The Poems Of January Bogotá, 1951
Poetry Medellin, 1951
Words Of Absence Manizales, 1953
Minimum Key Manizales, 1965
My Own Words Manizales, 1986
Time To Live Bogotá, 1992
Bell Of Rain Commemorative Edition Manizales, 1997
Shadow Of Love Roldanillo, 1998
The Names Of Absence Bogotá, 2006
All That Was Mine Bogotá, 2008
Puzzl Bogotá, 2010
Memory Time Ibague, 2010
All Love Looking For My Heart Madrid, 2012
The Simple Truth That I Love You Madrid, 2012

Nonfiction:
Popayan Backwater City, Popayan, 1956.

Awards and honors:
Culture's Grand Order, Culture Ministry of Colombia
Simon Bolivar Medal, National Education Ministry of Colombia
Artistic Merit Honor Medal, Mayoralty of Bogotá, D.C.
Gabriela Mistral Order, Education Ministry of Chile
Villegas Aquilino Order, Government of Caldas
Manizales's Cross, Mayoralty of Manizales
Arts and Letters Award, Success Women Foundation
Erato Award, Corporation Art and Poetry in the Street, Sabaneta, Antioquia
The Life and Work Award, Culture Ministry of Colombia

HAZARA

Your name and your letters,

Hazara

the letters of your name

already part of my days

and my nights.

I think of the distant beauty of your people,

your colors, your flags

Green?? Blue?

tell me, how are your gods?

From here I seek for the face

of your children, your wives,

the elderly who have lived

all wars.

We are here waiting for peace

After half a century of violence.

Pray to your gods for us,

that I beg to mine

for peace and joy to Hazara.

HAZARA

Tu nombre y tus letras,

Hazara

las letras de tu nombre

ya forman parte de mis dias

y mis noches.

Pienso en la lejana belleza de tu pueblo,

en sus colores, en sus banderas

¿verde?¿azul?

cuèntame, ¿còmo son tus dioses?

Desde aquì busco el rostro

de tus niños, de tus mujeres,

de los ancianos que han vivido

todas las guerras.

Aquì estamos esperando la paz

despuès de medio siglo de violencia.

Ruega a tus dioses por nosotros,

que yo ruego al mìo

por la paz y la alegrìa de Hazara.

Nyein Way
Myanmar

Nyein Way is a poet, writer, and educator. He performs poetic texts, writes articles about poetry and education, and leads poetry workshops inside and outside of Myanmar.

He participated in the Mekong Project in 2004 in Phenom Penh, contributed an article about Myanmar theatre in The *Encyclopedia of Asian Theatre* by Greenwood Publishing in 2008, which won the best reference book prize from The American Library Association.

Nyein has appeared at poetry readings in Yangon, Santa Fe (New Mexico USA), Los Angeles, and published a poetry anthology, *Within 20 Years* in 2005. He published an educational book in 1999. Nyein read poetry with the most famous theatre troupe in Myanmar, Shwe Man Chan, with the Thai theatre troupe at Independence Day Festival at the football field of Hlaing Township, Yangon, collaborating with the performance *Philosophy Tree* by New York-based Thai Dancer'Khun Pichet, artist Myat Kyawt and Shwe Man Chan Tha on January 3, 2009.

PEACE

is not a word but a word

is not poetry but a poem

is not crying but a cry

is not warring but a war of social justice

through a

frag   ment   ed

and

(*annotated*)

life voyage.

Gaston Bellemare
Québec

Gaston Bellemare is the President & Founder of the International Poetry Festival (Festival International de la Poésie). This festival is an international event which attracts more than 40,000 people from all ages and walks of life. Every year, the ten-day Festival features over 350 events and welcomes over 100 poets from the five continents in seventy chosen locations in and around Trois-Rivières, making it the Poetry Capital.

Gaston co-founded the Écrits des Forges, was the poetry publishing house's treasurer from 1971 to 1983 before presiding over it from 1983 to 2008. The publisher had over 1,200 book titles on catalogue and jointly published 500 titles with fifty-one different publishing houses in seventeen countries. On average, fifty titles came out each year.

Current professional activities
Having chaired the Association Nationale des Éditeurs de Livres (National Association of Publishers) from 2004 to 2008, and again from 2010 to 2012, he has now been named publisher emeritus. He is also the president of Copibec (2008-2009, 2010-2011, 2012-2013), of the Festival International de la Poésie (since 1985), of the Saint-Denys-Garneau Foundation (since 2004), is a member of the board of directors of the Fondation des Parlementaires (Parliamentary Foundation), of the Commission de Droit de Prêt Public (Public Lending Right Commission) and of the Bibliothèque et Archives Nationales du Québec (Quebec's National Archives and Library), and he sits on numerous cultural juries.

Gaston is a leader and unifier. He first expressed his passion for poetry by writing the very first book published by the Écrits des Forges. He invested time and money into promoting poetry and cultural publishing. He also created ten poetry prizes including the Festival International de la Poésie's Grand Prix Quebecor, dreamed up the Promenade de la Poésie (300 poems posted on the city's walls) and co-founded the Promenade Internationale de la Poésie with Maryse Baribeau (101 poems from 101 authors from forty-three countries in French and twenty-one other languages).

In 2001, he founded the Fédération des festivals internationaux de poésie (the Federation of International Poetry Festivals or FFIP) which allowed him to create an informal network of festivals that follows the UNESCO curriculum. He also instigated cooperation agreements and partnerships with 20 international poetry festivals. More recently, Gaston Bellemare has received the Order of Canada (2013).

Speaking Hazara
to tell a different world.

Each people
Is part
of the world's eternity

Parler Hazara
dire différemment le monde

Les différences d'âme
sont l'éternité des peuples.

Zohra Hamid
South Africa

Hamid is a member of the "Dancing Pencils" writing club and an educator and social worker currently employed at the Daydawn Special School in Durban, South Africa. She has had two poems published by the Christian Poetry Association.

WHY

"Rover" "Chocolate"and "Nunooz"
Bark at each other to make
Themselves understood
I don't undetstand what they
They are saying because they
Speak another language
Why? Because they are 'dogs'

We are fortunate we have
The power of language
And can communicate with
Each other . Why then? Is there
War in Iraq Violence and bloodshed
In Israel and Palestine
Terror and atrocities on the Hazara People

I don't understand
Is it because we have forgotten
The human language of
Love undestanding and
Compassion
Or is the human race no longer

'Human"

Please God Help me to
Understand this wonnderful and
Beautiful creation which man
Has despoiled
Please restore my faith in
HUMAN -KIND

LAND OR AIR

They don't need a passport
Visa or permission to go
Anywhere in the world

Birds have outsmarted us
In their simplicity
Weather is their only fear

They can go to Australia Iran
Pakistan Norway or Afghanistan
No need for acceptance or
Rejection
No need to be treated as outcasts
Or aliens

They just soar higher and
Higher
Whilst we poor earthlings stay
Stuck to the ground in our
Parasitic claim to dust and soil

Fly , pretty bird spread your
Wings and let us poor earthlings
Envy you

Amir Or
Israel

Amir Or is the author of eleven volumes of poetry in Israel and thirteen volumes in Europe and America. His poems have been published in more than forty languages. Amir has received several poetry prizes, among them the Levi Eshkol Prime Minister's Prize, Fulbright Award for Writers, the Bernstein Prize, and the Oeneumi Poetry Prize.

He has been awarded fellowships from the University of Iowa, Oxford University, and the Heinrich Boll Foundation among others. His translations into Hebrew include *The Gospel of Thomas* and

Anthology of Erotic Greek Poetry. For his translations he received the Minister of Culture Prize.

Amir studied philosophy and comparative religion at the Hebrew University in Jerusalem, and lectured there on Ancient Greek Religion. He has taught creative writing in Israel, Europe, and the US. In 1990 he founded the Helicon Society. He has been Editor-in-Chief of Helicon's journal and poetry books and set up the Arabic-Hebrew Poetry School.

He is a member of the World Poetry Movement steering committee and of the European Association of Writing Programs. He serves as national coordinator of the U.N.-sponsored Poets for Peace and as national editor for the international poetry magazines *Atlas* and *Blesok*. He is the editor of Catuv poetry series.

THE BARBARIANS (ROUND TWO)

It was not in vain that we awaited the barbarians,

it was not in vain that we gathered in the city square.

It was not in vain that our great ones put on their official robes

and rehearsed their speeches for the event.

It was not in vain that we smashed our temples

and erected new ones to their gods;

as proper we burnt our books

that have nothing in them for people like that.

As the prophesy foretold the barbarians came,

and took the keys to the city from the king's hand.

But when they came they wore the garments of the land,

and their customs were the customs of the state;

and when they commanded us in our own tongue

we no longer knew when

the barbarians had come to us.

Translated by Vivian Eden
From *Plates from The Museum of Time* ArtAArk

הַבַּרְבָּרִים: סִבּוּב שֵׁנִי

לֹא לַשָּׁוְא חִכִּינוּ לַבַּרְבָּרִים,

לֹא לַשָּׁוְא נִקְהַלְנוּ בְּכִכַּר הָעִיר.

לֹא לַשָּׁוְא עָטוּ גְדוֹלֵינוּ אֶת בִּגְדֵי כְבוֹדָם

וְשִׂגְּבוּ אֶת נְאוּמָם לִכְבוֹד הַמְּאֹרָע.

לֹא לַשָּׁוְא בְּתַצְנוּ מְקֻדָּשֵׁינוּ

וּבָנִינוּ אֲחֵרִים לְאֵלֵיהֶם;

כַּדָּת שָׂרַפְנוּ אֶת סְפָרֵינוּ

אֲשֶׁר אֵין חֵפֶץ בָּם לַאֲנָשִׁים כָּאֵלֶּה.

כִּדְבַר הַנְּבוּאָה בָּאוּ הַבַּרְבָּרִים,

וְנָטְלוּ מִיַּד הַמֶּלֶךְ אֶת מַפְתְּחוֹת הָעִיר.

אַךְ בְּבוֹאָם עָטוּ לְבוּשׁ כִּלְבוּשׁ הָאָרֶץ,

וּמִנְהָגָם הָיָה מִנְהַג הַמְּדִינָה;

וְעֵת צִוּוּ עָלֵינוּ בִּלְשׁוֹנֵנוּ,

לֹא יָדַעְנוּ עוֹד מָתַי

בָּאוּ הַבַּרְבָּרִים.

קשב 2012 © אמיר אור, *משא המשוגע* מתוך

Ivan Djeparoski
Macedonia

Ivan "Ivica" Djeparoski (b.1958, Skopje, Republic of Macedonia) is a philosopher, cultural theorist, poet, and translator. He graduated from the Faculty of Philosophy in Skopje where he received his M.A. and Ph.D.

Ivan is an author of twelve books in the field of aesthetics and cultural theory and also of five poetry books, for which he was awarded the "Mlad Borec Prize" (1984), "Dimitar Mitrev Prize" (1993), and "Paradigm Prize" (2009). He works at the Faculty of Philosophy in Skopje as a professor of "Aesthetics," "History of Aesthetics" and "Philosophy of Culture." He was Head of the Institute of Philosophy (2005-2009) and secretary of Macedonian P.E.N. Centre, (1999-2001; 2009- present). He has also translated numbers literary works (W. Blake, Y. Brodsky, J. Joyce, D. Hume, and E. Burke). In 1993, Igor was granted the "Grigor Prlicev Award" for a poetic rendition. His poetry and some of his essays have been translated into several languages.

UNHEIMLICH*

Is it possible that I've recently become homeless at home
In our happy Europe only through fear that
Sooner or later, what was suppressed will return again?

Should I keep on dreaming of my own freedom
Away from the fragile home, at an age when many
Find themselves attracted to the calmness of the eternal resting place?

My fear of being influenced by those from the other side of reality
Is not just a matter of poetic or philosophical influence,
But a fear that I am already *Beyond the Pleasure Principle*.

A play of repetition as the play of existence:
I and Europe, Europe and I. You and Europe, Europe and you.
Ritual circling. Dizziness.

An ideal love towards being homeless at home!
 *Unheimlich – literally "un-home-ly", but idiomatically, "scary", "creepy", "uncanny" is a Freudian concept of an instance where something can be familiar, yet foreign at the same time, resulting in a feeling of it being uncomfortably strange.

Attila F. Balázs
Slovakia

Attila F. Balázs, Hungarian writer, poet, literary translator, and publisher was born in Targu Mures (Transylvania) on January 15th, 1954. He studied at the Theological College in Alba Iulia between 1973-1976. In 1977 he studied librarian specialization and literary translation in Bucharest, where he graduated in 1988.

Since 1990 Attila has lived in Slovakia. In 1994 he established the publishing house *AB-ART*, and since then he has been the company director. Attila is the general editor of the literary journal *Szőrös Kő*, and has received several literary awards (Madach, Lucian Blaga, and Eminescu).

Atilla is a member of the Slovakian, Hungarian, and Romanian writers' organizations and the Hungarian PEN Club Vice President.

Many of his poems and short stories have been translated into English, Romanian, Czech, Slovakian, Slovenian, Serbian, Macedonian, Albanian, Spanish, Portuguese, Swedish, and French.

His major works include:
Masks, Poems – 1992, Madách, Bratislava.
The Juice of the Cat, Short Stories– 1992, Microgramma, Bratislava.
Naked Knights, Selected and New Poems– 2002, AB-ART, Bratislava.
My Cross of Words 50 Years 50 Poems– 2004, Lilium Aurum, D. Streda.
Transformations of Casanova– Premeny Casanovu. Bilingual (Hungarian-Slovakian) Edition.
Missa Bestialis, Poems translated into Romanian by A. Iancu – 2008, AB-ART, Bratislava.
Escape from the Ghetto, Literary translations—2008. AB-ART, Bratislava.
A Bag of Cherries, Contemporary Romanian Poetry—2009, AB-ART, Bratislava.
Poems – Poezii – Bilingual, (Hungarian – Romanian) edition,--2009, Limes, Cluj.
Minimal, Poems-- 2010 AB-ART, Bratislava.
Casanova's Metamorphoses, Short Stories in Romanian—2011, Grinta, Cluj.
Blue, Poems-- *2011, AB-ART, Bratislava.*
Minimal, Poems in German—2011, Gabriele Schaefer Verlag, Herne.
Casanova's Metamorphoses, Short Stories-- 2012. AB-ART.
Gordiev Jazol, Poems in Macedonian—2012 Matica Skopje.
The Scene, (Multilingual Anthology) -- 2012, Orient-Occident, Bukarest.
Prelomljeni hleb, Poems in Serbian--2012, Libertatea, Pančevo.
Beautiful, Poems-- 2013, AB-ART, Bratislava.
Minimal Poems in Portuguese, translated by José Eduardo Degrazia, Editora Aty--2013, Porto Alegre, Brazilia.
Casanova's Metamorphoses, Short Stories in English, translated by Adrian George Sahlean, 2013, Ekstasis Editions, Canada

STATUESQUE STUBBORNNESS

you no longer wonder

at the dolphin leaps of great thoughts

the rippling of fears behind walls

the acid and implacable bite of hatred

when bubbling it dissolves

the harmonious forms

the tear that has collected in the corner of your eyes evaporates

before

dissolving the dust of centuries

which has nestled in your pores

accenting the gloominess of your features

your statuesque stubbornness

you forgot to cry in the grotesque time

HISTORY

the plaster flakes off the facade

a little boy picks up the little finger broken off from a stone statue

lying on the dirty street and

throws it into the basin of a fountain

the pigeon shit covers the ornaments with a dull patina

it clatters, honks its horns, its sirens scream, laugh, curse

mingling with pleasant and unpleasant noises

on the street, behind the walls, on the walls, in the walls,

in you, in me, in everyone, history

how long can they get along with each other

for how long will they complement, shape

each other peacefully?

Forgiveness, like a faded set design full of cracks,

was lost among the junk under the feet

he may have just thrown it like a pebble into the murky waters of the fountain

the bored little boy while tired of life the statue on the façade of the building gets ready to leap to its death

Ioana Trica
Romania

Ioana Trică, was born in Grindu, Romania. She graduated from the University of Bucharest, focusing on the Romanian and French languages. A poet and translator, she has been publishing since 1999 in magazines and books, original poems and translations from French and Rhaeto-Romansh (a Latin idiom spoken in Switzerland with only a few tens of thousands of speakers). She calls attention to the Rhaeto-Romansh literature and culture, whose language is protected by UNESCO.

Ioana's work has appeared in journals and anthologies in France, Canada, Argentina, and Spain. She has published several volumes of poetry and translations: *Someone Else*, Suspended *Continents*, *El Tiempo Con Rostro Extraño Sleep Crusades*, and *An Island in the North*, among others.

She has been a member of the PEN French Club since 2008. Her poems are translated in Spanish, French, Catalan, and Albanian. Her books include *Someone Else*, 2005; *Suspended Continents*, 2008; *El Tiempo Con Rostro Extraño*, 2008 *Sleep Crusades*, 2011; *An Island in the North*, 2013.

THE CHERRY TREE'S TIME OF FIRE

Here is the cherry tree's time of fire
and the space
where you lock yourself
as in an unsafe night

between loser and winner
pain is equally divided
as is death

in war you can only be defended by
your own shadow

no reward for the winner
no consolation to the defeated

But here comes the time of fire
of the cherry tree.

Translation: Patricia Lidia

ORA DE FOC A CIREȘULUI

Iată ora de foc a cireșului
și spațiul
în care te-nchizi
ca într-o noapte nesigură

între învins și-nvingător
durerea se-mparte egal
ca și moartea

în război te poate apăra doar
propria umbra

nici o răsplată pentru învingător
nici o mângâiere pentru cel învins

dar iată vine iar ora de foc
a cireșului.

Michaël Glück
France

Michaël Glück is a French poet, prose-writer, playwright, and translator. He received the Prix de Créateurs in 1981 for *La mémoire écorchée/Abbatoirs La Mouche* (Editions Jean-Michel Place). *Cette chose-là, ma mère* (Editions J. Brémond) received the Prix Antonin Artaud. Glück, who studied philosophy with Emanuel Levinas, has evolved a distinctive Judaic vision within the context of modern French poetry.

even when we have so few words

we are still alive

we can walk

we can walk and talk

we can give hands and words

we can say

every people needs words

every people needs his own language

as every poet

every people is a poet

you and you and I

I go

I walk

one foot after another foot

my feet are dancing on the earth

I ear your songs

I see you dancing

and nobody can forbid you

to go there where

your people gives a breath

to your poems

you are still alive

we need every people

we need every life every

language every song

nobody reigns

blood is blood

beat of human hearts

Quito Nicolaas
The Netherlands

Eclips Politico/Political Eclipse (poetry) Uitgeverij Charuba, 40 pag/1990.
Ilusion Optico/Optical Illusion (poetry), Uitgeverij Charuba, 50 pag/1995.
Destino/Destiny (poetry), Uitgeverij Excalibur, 70 pag/2000.
Gerede Twijfels/Reasonable Doubts(poetry), Uitgeverij Excalibur, 103 pag/ 2002
Tera di Silencio/Land of Silence (novel), Uitgeverij Excalibur, 312 pag/ 2004.

Atardi di Antaño/Yesterday's Evenings (poetry), Uitgeverij SL, 150 pag/2005.
Alameda (short stories), Uitgeverij SL, 120 pag/2008.
Verborgen leegte/Hidden Emptyness (novel), BookIsh Publishers, 325 p./2010.
Bos pa Planta/Constructing Voices (poetry), BookIsh Publishers, 2011.
Sombra di recuerdo/Shadow memories (novel)), BookIsh Publishers, 2013.

Lectures
Dichters onder de zon/*Poets under the sun*,
  Cultureel Centrum Corossia, Almere, 15 november 2006.
Papiamentstalig proza/ Papiamento Prose,
  University of Amsterdam, 23 april 2007
Eeuwige stem uit het verleden/Ancient voices in the past,
  Den Haag, 16 november 2007.
Status Aparte: Politieke en literaire ontwikkeling,
  Almere, 16 maart 2008.
City of Hope, Writers & Poets in San Nicolas.
  Utrecht, 31 maart 2008.
Behind Literary Shadows
  In Between the Islands conference, Curaçao 5-9 nov. 2008
Historical novels: The Battle for the Reader.
  Internationaal symposium Historische romans, Amsterdam 19 september 2009.
The Rise of Migrant Literature.
  Caribbean Lagoon, Utrecht 6 december 2009.
How to Identify Aruban Literature.
  University of St. Martin, 5 juni 2010

BETRAYAL

So much bloodshed between
peoples who lived peacefully
for centuries
in their village.

Only their appearance differed
that of another ethnicity
In their Hazara music and folklore
Their habits, their everyday rights.

Done everything to emancipate
not for others but for ourselves.
The power of any man which
glorifies in length of years.

Living in fear
childhood friends who betray you
at the negotiating table
they will spit on us.

So many divisions

to give the floor to arms

bodies that no longer

give substance to ideas.

CONVERSATIONS

At the table, he drifts around me
without a fixed location
cores filling with lives of others.
As no other rightly at long last,
after being months in the mountains
afraid of what I have always feared.

My youth I don't wanna repeat.
from all that frightening noise, I went deaf.
silence I only knew afther my birth.
The noise that still plagued my spirit.
car tyres on a burning neck; screeming and tears.

Our village hardly recognizable after all these destruction
Everything bombed, shops, buildings, schools … my youth.
My body freezing of the past,
deadly silence along all those dead bodies,
friends in my memory: rigid and spoiled.

Here I'm again, without a fixed location
along a river, under a roof of rain
enough to welcome the hours in days
in a valley that separated life from each other,
where my own blood could no longer flows.

With my body, eyes and memory
floating ,between death bodies, on wuthering waters
from frontier to port, from region to city.
The suffering did still not turned their backs,
as teenager deprived of my second skin.

Noria Adel
Algeria

Noria Adel is a photographer and poet born in Algiers, Algeria. She was an invited poet to the Poetry Festival "Les Voix de la Méditerranée" in Lodeve, France, and was a Laureate Artist of UNESCO's 2012 Aschberg Bursaries for Artists.

Recent publications include:
- *Les Voix de la Méditerranée* - Anthologie poétique, Éditions La passe du vent, France, 2013.
- *Damas / Alger: l'Allumeur de réverbères, Histoires minuscules des révolutions arabes,* Chèvre-feuille étoilée, France, 2012.
- *Youss veillera le marais: Acte poétique d'un gardien,* Al Bait, Algiers, 2009.
- *Entorse géométrique*, Mille Feuilles, Algiers, 2009.

The History is long seated in the bluish depths of an endless look
The story of a mountain that striates a heavy sky and shades rosy cheeks
The story of faces defying dark hearts of those who do not see them
While the large sky breeds men who are stretched like dry sails
When they don't cover
They fly.

Que l'histoire est longue assise dans les profondeurs bleuâtres d'un regard sans fin
L'histoire d'une montagne qui strie un ciel lourd et ombre des joues roses
Celle de visages qui défient les obscurs cœurs de ceux qui ne les voient pas
Lorsque le large ciel niche des hommes tendus comme des voiles secs qui s'envolent même s'ils ne couvrent pas.

Francisco Sánchez Jiménez
Colombia

Francisco Sánchez Jiménez was born in Bogotá, Colombia, South America. He studied in the Washington School, where he received a baccalaureate. Francisco graduated from the law school at the Universidad Nacional of Colombia. He has been a writer since 1984.

HAZARA IN MY THOUGHTS

Hazara in my thoughts:
For my tongue
Now there is a stabbing
word: Hazara.
Desert in a wind of blood
Voice with a scar of mountains
and brothers on the route
of death.
The force of horror
has held, Hazara,
all languages
in order to impoverish you.
And multiple murderers' faces have
filled the childhood
dream and
tried to undermine
the beautiful face of the
women.

If it were possible from
solitude,
my distant friendship
loves as you do,
Hazara,

and aims to know

a victory

possessing the letters of

your name.

HAZARA EN MI PENSAMIENTO

Para mi lengua

ahora existe una palabra

lancinante: Hazara.

Desierto en un viento de sangre

Voz con cicatriz de montañas

y hermanos en la ruta

de la muerte.

La fuerza del horror

ha tenido, Hazara,

todos los idiomas

para esquilmarte.

Y los múltiples rostrosde los asesinos han

colmado el sueño

de la infancia e

intentado socavar

el bello rostro de las

mujeres.

Si fuera posible desde

la soledad

mi lejana amistad

ama lo mismo que usted,

Hazara,
y aspira saber de
una victoria
que posea las letras de
tu nombre.

Werewere Liking
Cameroon/ Ivory Coast

Werewere Liking was born May 1st, 1950 in Cameroon. She is a prolific writer, having written novels, plays, short stories, essays and books of art and poetry. She has been painting since 1968, participating in many art expositions across the world. In 1985 she founded the artistic group Ki-Yi Mbock, and has directed and acted in more than thirty plays and spectacles that have toured the world with Ki-Yi Mbock.

Werewere is the founder and president of the Pan-African Foundation Ki-Yi for the Foundation for Youth and Creativity and Cultural Development. Liking is one of two lead singers of the group "Les Reines Mères" ("The Queen Mothers") who have released three albums. As of July 2004, she has been a permanent member of the Academy of Science, African Cultures, and African Diasporas.

Prizes:
Noma Prize, 2005
Book of the Year 2007, for "La Memoire Amputée"
"Faiseuse de Paix," 2009
Commander of the Order of Merit of the Ivory Coast, 2013

"I AM LOVE" SAY THE VOICES IN THE BELLIES OF WOMEN

1

Enough of hate

Enough of Racism

Enough of extremisms

Enough of exclusionisms

There's only one Human Race

Not like with the animals

Where there are Bipeds

And Quadrupeds

Canines

And felines

Crawlers

And fliers

Molluscs

And fishes

2

The color of the skin,
Of the hair or the eyes
Isn't enough to classify
Human beings of different races

The complication of skin
Which leads some to underrate themselves
Should absolutely be surpassed
For the sake of a better humanity
The Spirit unifies colors and genders
And transcends Times and Spaces

        FORGET HATRED, I AM LOVE

3

MORE THAN "UNDER DEVELOPED"

Nobody can be all poor

Penniless you can be rich in dignity

Nobody can be all rich

Loaded with gold you can be poor in generosity

We humans all are rich

But each one misses something

That another among us possesses in abundance

By enriching ourselves all together

We'll banish all discriminations

"Developed" or called "under developed"

It's all of humanity which has to evolve

In order finally to recover a just happiness

And the loftiness of being Human Beings, Divine

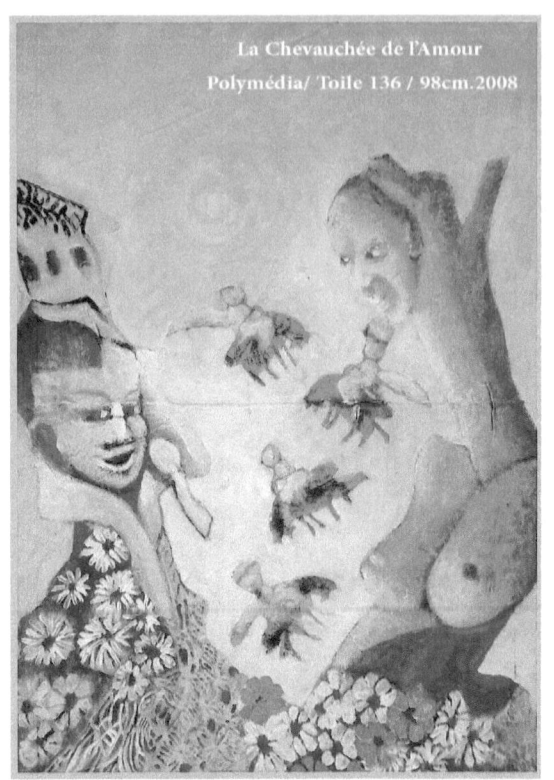

OU «SUIS L'AMOUR» DISENT LES VOIX DE VENTRES DE FEMMES...

Assez de haine

Assez de Racisme

Assez d'extrémismes

Et d'exclusionnismes

Il y a une seule Race Humaine

Pas comme chez les animaux

Où il y a des Bipèdes

Et des Quadrupèdes

Des Canins

Et des félins

Des Rampants

Et des Volants

Des mollusques

Et des poissons ...

NON' GWÉHA: «SUIS L'AMOUR» (suite)

La couleur de la peau,

Des cheveux ou des yeux

Ne suffit pas pour classer

Les humains en différentes races

Le complexe de la peau

Qui conduit certains à se sous estimer

Doit absolument être dépassé

Pour une meilleure humanité

L'Esprit unifie couleurs   et sexes

Et transcende le Temps   et les Espaces

OUBLIE LA HAINE, SUIS L'AMOUR

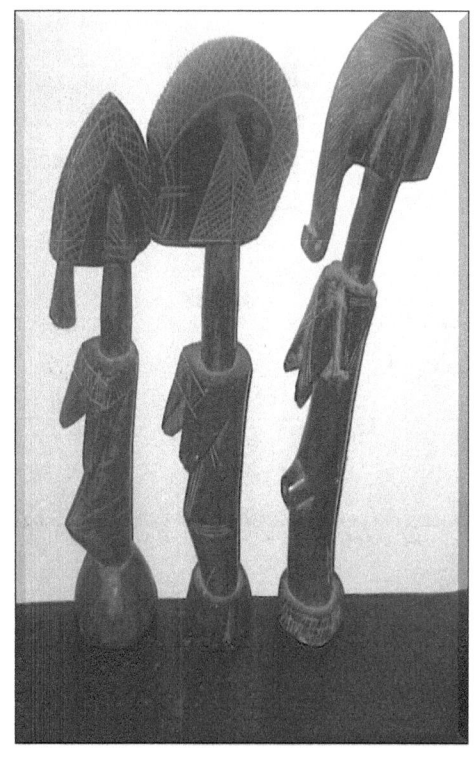

PLUS DE «SOUS DÉVELOPPÉS»

Nul ne peut être pauvre de tout

Pauvre d'argent tu peux être riche de dignité

Nul ne peut être riche de tout

Riche d'or tu peux être pauvre de générosité

Humains nous sommes tous riches

Mais manquons chacun de quelque chose

Qu'un autre parmi nous possède à foison

En nous enrichissant les Uns des Autres

Nous bannirons toutes les discriminations

« Développés » ou dits «sous développés»

C'est l'humanité tout entière qui doit évoluer

Pour enfin retrouver un bonheur équitable

Et la fierté d'être Humains, Divins…

Beppe Costa
Italy

Beppe is an editor, poet, writer, bookseller, and a cultural promoter. He has devoted his life to books. In 1976 he founded the publishing house Pellicanoblibri. He has written several books of poetry and won the Alfonso Gatto prize for "Impaginato per affeto" His latest publications include *Anche Ora Che La Luna* and *Rosso*.

Beppe has collaborated with various magazines such as *RaiUno Radio*, *Giornale del Sud*, *I Siciliani*, and the Gironale *di Sicilia* as a reporter.

In 2012 and 2013 he participated in the Galilee at the International Festival of Nissan. He received the Career Award at the International Prize City of Ostia. Currently, he directs the book series *Inediti rari e diversi* for SEAM Editions while living in Rome.

HEROIN/HEROINE

heroine is not heroic

dies soon as the day breaks

with all, even if few

hopes learn

a world that lash

and punishes alone

has no eyes and loses

sunrises and sunsets

although other human beings

know, we, the people

helpless we remain losers

extreme minority of minorities

William Pérez Vega
Puerto Rico

William is a writer, educator, environmentalist, activist for just causes and of everything that constitutes a claim by the marginalized ones. He has published over sixteen titles, including *Daily Verses* (1987), *That's the Cry* (1998), *Rainbow* (1990), *Nanas and Verse* (2002), *Song for You* (2004), *The Death of the Gods* (2007), *My Singing Lesson is Done* (2008), and *Areíto* (2010).

He has also published in poetry *Anthologies to be Sung* (1984), *New Puerto Rican Decimario* (1989), and *The Green Book International Poetry Festival of Puerto Rico* (2011).

Part of William's work has been incorporated into various musical productions. Has has participated in several international poetry festivals, and is a member of the Board of Directors of the International Poetry Festival of Puerto Rico. His poetry is powerful, simple, full of social content, and very committed.

I HAVE ONLY WORDS

In support of the Hazara

I want one verse to break chains

to stop fire and shrapnel,

to relieve pain and wipe away tears,

to dip the thirst of your lips

and then give birth to the earth and deserts

that shelters all nudity

down to the bones of the soul

A verse that blows fire

on all oppressors

that undoes the ties of shame

to draw different ways

to the horn of plenty

to bury the common grave of oblivion

and undo indifference

to erase all borders

I want a verse that rains

milk and honey on your face

at three in the afternoon

that makes a shroud in every cry

and draws smiles and flowers

to fill the table,

one verse where freedom

William Pérez Vega

is flesh and blood justice

But I have only a handful of letters

dressed as a watchword

and my rifle of verses and hopes.

SOLO TENGO PALABRAS

Quiero un verso que rompa cadenas
que detenga el fuego y las metrallas,
que alivie los dolores y enjugue llantos,
que moje la sed de tus labios
y haga parir la tierra y los desiertos
que abrigue todas las desnudeces
hasta los huesos del alma

Un verso que sople fuego
sobre todos los opresores
que deshaga las ataduras de la ignominia
que dibuje caminos diferentes
hasta el cuerno de la abundancia,
que sepulte la fosa común del olvido
y deshaga indiferencias
hasta borrar todas las fronteras

Quiero un verso que llueva
leche y miel sobre tu rostro
que llovizne café tibio a las tres de la tarde
que haga de sudario en cada llanto
y dibuje sonrisas y flores
hasta llenar la mesa,
un verso donde la libertad

sea justicia de carne y hueso

Pero solo tengo un puñado de letras
vestidas de consigna
y mi fusil de versos y esperanzas.

December evening-
grandmother and baby watch
the Evening star

Angelee Deodhar

Angelee Deodhar
India

Angelee Deodhar is an eye surgeon by profession. She is also a haiku poet, translator and artist. Her haiku/haiga have been published internationally in several books, journals and on the Internet. To promote haiku in India she has translated six books of haiku from English to Hindi.

Bilingual books published:
If Someone Asks . . . Masaoka Shiki's Life and Haiku, 2005.
Classic Haiku: A Master's Selection, edited by Miura Yuzuru, 2006.
Ogura Hyakunin Isshu: 100 Poems by 100 Poets, 2007.
Children's Haiku from around the World–A Haiku Primer, 2007.
Indian Haiku, 2008.
The Distant Mountain , Kobayashi's Isaa's Life and Haiku, 2009.

THE ROAD TO BAMYAN

I, a Hazara,
homeless nomad
walk in snow above the clouds
to Bamyan...

where the faceless Buddhas guard
the caves of my ancestors

I await the almond flowers of spring
to cover the graves of
the tens of thousands
killed on the way
to the promised land

I, a Hazara,
homeless nomad
walk in snow above the clouds...

come walk with me,
hold my hand
guide me now
as my faltering steps slow
              on the road to Bamyan...

Fanny Moreno
Colombia

Fanny Moreno was born on September 4, 1946 in Medellín, Antioquia, Colombia, and South America.

She studied to become a Commercial Bilingual Secretary and worked as a secretary for many years. She is now retired. She has won several awards in poetry and fiction writing, mostly abroad (Colombia, U.S.A, Spain, Uruguay, Brazil).

Fanny has published two books, one of poetry titled *Búsqueda (Search)*, and other of short stories entitled *"Ensueños" (Daydreams)*. She is currently writing a new book about her memories and thoughts, aimed at teenagers.

She is a member of The Cove Rincon International Poetry & Other Arts of Miami, L'Art International of West Palm Beach, Florida. She is a founding member of the Workshop "Uraba Escribe" (Uraba Writes) and while living in Miami she participated in the United Seniors Association of America. In October 2010 she attended the Eighth Congress of Women Poets from Antioquia.

Fanny has been included in several literary readings and anthologies of both poetry and fiction. Currently she belong to the literature workshop Aluna in Antioquia, led by the internationally known poet, Marga López. Her main hobbies are writing, reading, photography, and handcrafts. She hase two daughters and one grandson. Her father passed away at 68, and her mother is still alive; she's 92. At present I'm writing her memoirs.

SILENT WAR

Our whole world is always preparing
for many kinds of wars,
and my fragile heart has already started
its own, and saddest war.
It is fighting alone and has no weapons;
It is fighting once more without support.
It is suffering for the Hazara people
and many others who have no more a place,
not a safe roof or even a little piece of bread.
My heart is fighting, Yes! but full of hope
those humans will wake up from their indolence
and finally will do what should be done
from the beginning of the times:
To love their brothers, our brothers,
no matter what they're coming from;
from the jungles, the deserts or the poles!
While our children march to face the enemy
I'm not clear about where I should be.
My heart is fighting! Nobody seems to notice,
his broken pieces flying to the sun
carrying my prayers to the hands of God
praying for my Hazara brothers,
For them to finally have peace!

April 19, 2013

John Curl
USA

John Curl is the author of eleven books of poetry, a memoir, and several volumes of history. Yoga Sutras of Fidel Castro is his latest poetry book. Ancient American Poets contains his translations and biographies of poets from ancient Native American Inca, Maya, and Aztec languages. He represented the USA at the World Poetry Festival of 2010 in Caracas, Venezuela. He is vice president of PEN Oakland, and a member of the Revolutionary Poets Brigade. He received a 2013 book award from Artists Embassy International. His Collected Poems 1967-2012 are in Revolutionary Alchemy, with a foreword by Jack Hirschman, poet laureate emeritus of San Francisco, who wrote, "John Curl has earned a place… among the foremost revolutionary American poets since the end of World War II."

HOW LONG HAZARA

How long can a rose bloom before its petals fall?
How long can a wild dog wail?
How long must I love you before you return my love?
How long must I wait until
my leaking ship begins to sail?

How long will the moon eclipse the sun?
How long will famine shriek?
How long will drought parch the barren soil?
How long will the world look the other way
while the powerful oppress the weak?

How long can a stone arch support a collapsing wall?
How long before the glaciers melt into the sea?
How long will it take for the plague to run its course?
How long must a people suffer
just for being who they will always be?

Kevin Kiely
Ireland

Kevin Kiely was born in County Down, North Ireland. He is a poet, novelist, playwright, and a literary critic as well as an American Fulbright Scholar with a PhD in modernist poetry.

Books: *Quintesse* (St Martin's Press, New York)
Mere Mortals
Plainchant for a Sundering
Breakfast with Sylvia, winner of the Patrick Kavanagh fellowship 2006
Francis Stuart: Artist and Outcast (Official Biography)
The Welkinn Complex
Patron to Modernist and Postmodernist Poetry at the Woodberry Poetry Room, Harvard

Selected Anthology Listings: *Something Sensational To Read in the Train* (anthology foreword: Brendan Kennelly) Lemon Soap Press, Dublin 2005; *Catullus: One Man of Verona* anthology ed. Ronan Sheehan Farmar & Farmar Ltd 2010; *Ends & Beginnings* anthology eds John Gery and William Pratt AMS Press Inc, New York 2011; 'A Map of Melancholy (long poem) in *Windows Anthology* eds. Heather Brett and Noel Monahan 2012; *In Place of Love and Country* eds Richard Parker & John Gery Crater Press, London 2013.

Plays on RTÉ:
Children of No Importance
Multiple Indiscretions.
Fiction for Young Readers:
SOS Lusitania O'Brien Press 2013
A Horse Called El Dorado (Bisto Award)

WE ARE WINOS!

The broken window pane is a spider's web design
And the river that cools the almighty city
While you pour the medicine. 'We are winos!'
You say, and we drink, mirrored in glass, water,
lakes and rivers…each silver drop of rain is
a spy-hole…all these journeys to your amber
lit city by night, each bridge is a span of thought
moving like the train, moving away from and yet
towards, aligned as well as parallel to the iron gold
bridge over the river to you. I am approaching
across a field where a hovering jet seeks the start
of a runway between the coloured lights, circus
lights of the airport, or cats-eyes on the roadway
twinned eyes, bright until passed, each cat in weeping
drizzle beneath the lingerie of night, scented in mist
but there is no straight way forward, philosophies
telling such slant tales tie movement down
in one dimension, the finite seems like a random
design, fixed on canvas in oils, set in mosaic,
filmed and in the can.

Therefore I drink you
as the pious used to swallow a rose-window of saints.
You stop the world when it does not explain itself.

This is our vision: the one which saves beyond
the ATMs, shelved items, the robot-pumps
the empty plastic sandwich pyramids…
Whereas, you and I in secret
for keeps and goodness amidst
this conflagration, this devastation
begin to adore the chaos, passing through
and whether they believe us or not—
Do we care? No. We are winos
of the resurrected crocus, the mahogany
nest in a tree awaiting leaves. The sun
in each drop of rain, the cats-eyes
that leap up from the darkness
the night without fear

Azam Abidov
Uzbekistan

AAZAM ABIDOV was born on November 8, 1974 in Namangan, City of Flowers, Uzbekistan and is a poet and translator. He trained in philology. He has several poetry and translation books to his credit. The most successful works by Aazam Abidov are *Tunes of Asia* (English translation of contemporary Uzbek poetry), *The Island of Anxiety* (poems in Uzbek, English, and Spanish), *Dream of*

Lightsome Dawns, *A Miracle Is On the Way* and *I leave you in complete boredom* (Uzbek translation of world poetry and fiction, as well as Aazam's own poems).

Azam writes in both Uzbek and English. His poems and translations have appeared in numerous anthologies in Uzbekistan, India, France, Korea, Japan, and Colombia and in many web magazines.

His awards include BBC World Uzbek Service's award for free speech in Uzbekistan (2005), and literary prizes from the "Ulughbek" Foundation (1996, 2000);

Azam was a winner of the Republican Contest for Uzbek and Uzbek Literature (1995), winner of the poetry contest "My First Booklet" for young poets and writers (1990) and winner of the competition "Art Holiday" (1987-1988).

Aazam's poems have been translated into Russian, Spanish, Assamese, Gujarati, Malayalam, Bulgarian, Turkish, Vietnamese, and Armenian, French, and Hindi languages. He was a Creative Writing Fellow at the University of Iowa (2004) and has attended poetry festivals, creative writing workshops, and cultural events in many countries.

A POEM OF EQUALITY

Who you are –
A white man,
black
or red,
You are a boon companion or a threat.
To put yourself first
how can you well afford,
 But look here –
 You're a human being from the Lord!

 Who you are –
A Muslim,
Christian,
Sikh,
You adore –
On men -
To play a trick,
With the others
will you not accord,
But remember,
 You're a human being from the Lord!

You are my brother,
You are my sister,

darling,

God will look at

not your varied colors, -

But at your heart

And at your good intentions

So, why kill each other,

Why fight,

We are equal

and we all have

the same right!

May God take

in due course

our lives.

Just tell me,

does friendship

have a price?

We were given time –

Very short

Remember,

we all return back to the Lord!

Who you are –

A white man,

black

or red,

You are a boon companion or a threat,

Pass these words
to others in a cord:
 We're ONE human being from the Lord!

Luis Galar

Poet, bookseller, cultural manager, Luis Galar performs work on the Internet, has studied philosophy, participated in documentary film productions. He is a supporter of plans for the improvement of social conditions for people-mediated education.

Luis' books of poetry include *Días y Sombras*, *Latir del Tiempo, Maimó, Gastada Voz,* and *Isla del hombre*. His work eminates from the question of good and evil: What is man, but all the good and the bad? Solving this gives evidence of the vices and customs of human nature, *poetizarlo*. The risk is confined to the history of a country where inequality, corruption and death are the order of the day.

RADIO

Dawn as every day. The dawn.

A radio broadcasts "bloody bitter battles"

my neighbor radio plays that,

regularly, without pause,

the words spoken

hit my ears like rough stones,

step into my body

run through my thickened blood,

diluting it, increasing my solitude;

look for some Bach, Toccata and Fugue ...

I increase the volume, I increase the volume, SUBO EL VOLUMEN

Somewhere's celebrating one death.

RADIO

Amanece, como todos los días amanece,

La radio   transmite *"cruentas acciones"*

eso emite la radio de mi vecino,

regularmente, sin pausa,

las palabras emitidas

golpean mis oídos como pedruscos

ingresan en mi cuerpo,

recorren mi espesa sangre,

diluyéndola, acrecentando mi soledad;

Busco algo de Bach, tocata y fuga…

Subo el volumen, subo el volumen, SUBO EL VOLUMEN

En algún lugar se festeja una muerte

Santiago B. Villafania
Philippines

Santiago B. Villafania is a bilingual Filipino poet who writes in English and in his native language of Pangasinan. He is the author of four poetry collections: *Bonsaic Verses* (CreateSpace, 2012), *Pinabli & Other Poems* (C&E Publishing/De La Salle University, 2012), *Malagilion: Sonnets tan Villanelles* (Komisyon sa Wikang Filipino, 2007), and *Balikas na Caboloan* (Voices from Caboloan, 2005) published by the National Commission for Culture and the Arts under its UBOD New Authors Series. His second book, *Malagilion* was a finalist in the 2007 National Book Award for Best Book of Poetry; and won the Gawad Komisyon (Gantimpalang Tamayo sa Tulang Pangasinan) for Pangasinan poetry in 2007.

"Villafania" has been published/anthologized in several countries and translated into several languages. He is one of the eleven Outstanding Pangasinenses and recipient of the 1st Asna Award for Arts and Culture (Literature) in 2010; and one of the Six Filipino Poets in "World Poetry Peace Festival" in Canada, 2013.

He is a member of the Philippine PEN and writes a regular weekly column for the "Sunday Punch."

SONNET TO A PILGRIM SOUL

for the Hazara people

When the sun gilds the sky in the morning
And deep darkness makes a noble retreat
O hear the music in the air fleeting
For you can never recapture the beat

When the morning spreads her warm golden wings
And the sapphire sky is wordlessly deep
Look yonder and feast with your eyes the things
Which you seldom see in your dreamful sleep

Don't you feel forlorn beloved pilgrim
If the world will mind your lowly a state
A time will come when their eyes will grow dim
And they too will fall on our self-same fate

An empty shell to decay into dust
When our days in the sun come into past

Althea Romeo-Mark
Antigua

Born in Antigua, West Indies, Althea Romeo-Mark is an educator who grew up in St. Thomas, US Virgin Islands. She has lived and taught in St. Thomas, the USA, Liberia, England and in Switzerland since 1991.

She was awarded the Marguerite Cobb McKay Prize by the Editorial Board of *The Caribbean Writer* in June, 2009. Her last poetry collection, *If Only the Dust Would Settle,* was published in 2009.

Althea has published in *St. Somewhere Journal, BLACKBERRY: a magazine, Persimmon Tree, The Caribbean Writer, The Antigua and Barbuda Review of Books,* KRITYA, *Off the Coast, Maine's International Poetry Journal,* Revista de Poesia Prometo: Memoria del XX Festival Internacional de Poesia de Medellin, *Dirtcakes, Tongues of the Ocean, Sea Breeze Journal of Contemporary Liberian Writings, Voodoo and Women.*

She has also been published in *Calabash: Journal of Contemporary Arts and Letters, Seasoning for the Mortar, The Hampden-Sydney Poetry Review, Kariba Fortella: An Anthology of Caribbean Short Stories, Tickling Along Free, Mini Sagas, Daily Telegraph, Yellow Cedars Blooming: An Anthology of Virgin Islands Poetry, Sisters of Caliban: Contemporary Women Poets in the Caribbean, Anthology of Pan-Caribbean Poetry, Liberia: Leben Wo der Pfeffer Wächts,* and *Revista Review Inter-Americana.*

THE FORSAKEN

for the Hazara people

We have dared to be "the other".
Outcasts in your eyes,
we threaten your world.
Your words are burning spears
seeking to pierce our armor.

Strength and wisdom repel
the weakening of faith and culture,
steel us against your witch-hunt,
steel us against the screams for our demise.

We seek respite, seek a haven
from the relentless hunt of our people.
We are not charlatans and terrorists.

We cannot return across rivers,
to crumbling villages,
cannot return to the scenes
of the cross-fired dead
and the burial of diseased animals.
That is an anathema.

We are Hazara!
We, too, are God's children.

May, 2013

Bengt Berg
Sweden

Bengt Berg was born in Torsby, Sweden, in 1946. He was first published in 1974 and has written more than 35 books, mostly poetry. Poems by Bengt have been translated into the Nordic languages as well as Arabic, Hebrew, English, German, Dutch, Greek, Spanish, Turkish, Polish, Slovakian, Russian, Latvian, Vietnamese, Malayalam and Hindi. He has been a member of the Swedish Parliament since 2010. His homepage is: www.heidruns.se.

TO MY HAZARA FRIENDS

Get ready for a new day
think about love a moment
Know thar the road ends
at the same place
as it once began

Stand still
waiting for the rain,
look for a circle in the grass
where we once stood
Cup your hand over
that spot, as for protection

Think about love, know
that rain will soon start
to fall; open hand

Luz Lescure
Panama

FEMICIDE

Where will the love of all go?
Where will happiness?
Why the fading smile
of those sad faces
of the slave and his sons,
of the homosexual, of God?
Is it that we do not understand
the darkness
covering our face, staining the life
and the cosmos so blue?
If I-You am the reason of being,
a primal tree,
a pink dragonfly flying in the park
the day of dawn,
also I-You am cloud,
morning dew, daily bread,
I am You-I, a
slave, prostitute, a miscarraige,
an angel of light;
if you kill her,
you'll be killing us all,
killing your reason for being,
you genocide of life,
murderer of God.

FEMICIDIO

¿Donde andará el amor de todos?
¿Donde la felicidad?
¿Por qué se desvanece la sonrisa
de aquellos rostros tristes
de la esclava y sus hijos,
del homosexual, de Dios?
¿Será que no entendemos
las tinieblas
que nos cubren el rostro, que nos tiñen la vida
y el cosmos tan azul?
Si yo-tu soy la razón de ser,
el árbol primigenio,
la libélula rosa que volaba en el parque
eldía del amanecer,
yo-tú soy nube
el rocío tempranero, el pan de cada día,
soy yo-tu,
esclava, prostituta, malparida,
ángel de luz,
si la matas a ella,
nos estás matando a todos,
matas tu razón de ser,
genocida de la vida,
asesino de tu Dios.

Lola Koundakjian
Armenia

Lola Koundakjian, a long time resident of New York City, writes in Armenian, her mother tongue and in English. She has organized evenings dedicated to the *Dead Armenian Poets' Society* since her university days, and has curated the online *Armenian Poetry Project* since 2006.

Lola has appeared in two international poetry festivals: Medallín, Colombia in 2010, and Lima, Peru, in 2013. In 2012, she co-edited with Catherine Fletcher an article for *Rattapallax* devoted to post-Genocide era Armenian poetry.

Her translations of modern Istanbul poets have been included in Dora Sakayan's newest edition of Western Armenian language teaching manual.

Lola is a 2011 and 2012 *Northern Manhattan Arts Alliance* grantee. Her first collection of poetry, *The Accidental Observer* appeared in 2011 and her second manuscript *Advise to a poet* was a finalist in Armenia's Orange Book Prize in 2012. Her work has appeared online and in print and has been translated into French, Spanish and Ukrainian

LIFE

She dices the onions finely.

A construction worker, 25, falls to his death.

She adds the coriander, cloves and ginger.

A soldier, 21, walks over a roadside bomb.

She removes the meatballs from the fridge

A journalist, 43, gets shot thru the head.

She stirs the sauce over a low fire

and adds a few tears to the pot.

Կեանք

Այս մէկը գործարանի մը մէջ մեռաւ 25 տարեկանին
Ուրիշ մը զինուոր, երրորդ մը կէթոյի մը մէջ նահատակ։
Կին մը շաբաթը եօթը օր կը սպասարկէ,
Քոյրը՝ ուրիշին զաւակները կը մեծցնէ։

Կեանքի հերոսներ՝
Ե՞րբ ձեր կարգին պիտ՝ հանգչիք,
Ո՞վ ձեր զաւակները կը մեծցնէ.
Ո՞վ ո՞վ ձեր մահուն կու լայ։

Zindzi Mandela
South Africa

Zindzi Mandela is a poet, businesswoman, and daughter of Nelson Mandela. She published her poetry book titled *Black as I Am* in 1978.

High Tide...Low Tide
I'm finding my rhythm
And keeping my flow

Wherever the current finds me
Is where I choose to go
Between a wave of darkness
And the crest of my glow

I'm finding my rhythm
And keeping my flow

My surf-board is my life-line
And every tumble my cry
The grateful breath of relief
Says my life is no lie

I'm finding my rhythm
And keeping my flow

Then Bambatha walked in
And I had no words
This shall be continued
No cutting these cords

Edvino Ugolini
Italy

Poet and Activist Edvino Ugolini was born in Trieste, Italy in 1950. He has published several books including the following:

- *Vita e Morte*, Nuovi Autori di Milano/ 1983.
- *Bagliori*, Antonio Giacomini di Udine/ 2000.
- *Poesie Ribelli*/ 2001.
- *Intrecci*/ 2003.
- *Tespi Editrice*/ 2009.

A collection of his poems titled *Incandescences* was translated by Jack Hirschman. This book was published in 2004.

YOU ARE NOT ALONE

A poem born to-day for the Hazara people and for all people of the world who are fighting for their freedom.

Under the stars of an enormous firmament

I have seen milions of men and women

Starving under the prepotence of the stronger

And begging for a bitch of freedom and dignity

In the indifference of the powerful of the world

Don't let the hope dying

Don't forget your origins

And hold on the fight for justice

Without justice your fight will be senseless

And our children will be not able to live

In world of PEACE and FRATERNITY

Sunday, April 07, 2013

NON SIETE SOLI

Sotto le stelle di un immane firmamento
Ho visto miriadi di uomini e donne
Annaspare sotto la prepotenza del più forte
E pregare per un po' di libertà e dignità
Nell'indifferenza dei potenti del mondo
Non lasciate morire la speranza
Non tradite le vostre origini
E tenete sempre alto il balauardo della giustizia
Senza giustizia la vostra lotta sarà vana
Ed i nostri figli non potranno vivere
In un mondo di PACE e FRATELLANZA

Jean-Claude Awono
Cameroon

Jean-Claude is president of the Poets' Circle and of the International Poetry Festival of the Seven Hills of the Yaoundé, Festival.

THE NEWS IS GOOD

For the Hazara people

Though the waves are speaking

Or one thinks of the dawn

The news is good

That things are going to the right

Or swinging to the left

The news is good

At the bloody end of the gun

Like at the entrance of a tunnel

The news is good

That the north's weeping

And the south sings it doesn't give a damn

The news is good

That one's keeping going

Or that one's stopped

The news is good

That one can say nothing or one can speak

That one might want it or refuse it

The news is good

Good or not

The news is good

And the wheel can turn

And the regime rest assured

LES NOUVELLES SONT BONNES

Quoique disent les ondes

Ou que pense l'aurore

Les nouvelles sont bonnes

Que les choses aillent à droite

Ou qu'elles virent à gauche

Les nouvelles sont bonnes

Au bout sanglant du fusil

Comme à l'entrée du tunnel

Les nouvelles sont bonnes

Que le nord pleure

Et le sud chante on s'en fout

Les nouvelles sont bonnes

Qu'on s'en aille

Ou que l'on reste

Les nouvelles sont bonnes

Qu'on se taise ou que l'on parle

Qu'on le veuille ou que l'on refuse

Les nouvelles sont bonnes

Bonnes ou pas bonnes

Les nouvelles sont bonnes

Et la roue peut tourner

Et le régime se rassurer

Stefania Battistella
Italy

Stefania Battistella was born in 1989 in Italy.

She published *Briciole di Pensieri e di Velluto* (AltroMondo publisher, 2010).

In 2011 Stefania moved to Rome and in the same year participated as a guest at the International Literary Festival City of Sassari, October in Poetry, with Jack Hirschman, Paul Polansky, Beppe Costa and others.

In 2012 and 2013, she participated at the "Nisan Festival", which takes place annually in Galilee. Her latest release is *L'amore m'ha fatto fragile*, Thauma Editions 2012.

HUMANS

humans

protagonists of books

that should burn

into the flames of intelligence

humans

without awareness

I wonder why nature

not rejecting them

humans

writing their end

without realizing

that will not be granted them

another nature to kill

Eugenia Sánchez Nieto
Colombia

Poet Eugenia Sánchez Nieto is from Colombia. She was born in Bogotá in 1953, and has published the following books of poetry:
Que Venga El tiempo Que Nos Prenda, Ulrika Editores, Bogotá, Colombia, 1985.
Con La Venia De Los Heliotropos, Ulrika Editores, Bogotá, Colombia, 1990.
Las Puertas De Lo Invisible, Centro Colombo Americano, Bogotá, Colombia,1993.
Visibles Ademanes, Colección Viernes de Poesía, Universidad Nacional, Bogotá, Colombia, 2004.

Dominios Cruzados, Colección 50 poetas Colombianos, Caza de Libros, Ibagué, Colombia, 2010.
Visibles Ademanes, Antología, Universidad Externado de Colombia, Julio 2013.

SCARS

The red spot on the black earth grows out of control

thousands of mouths cry after a black veil

skin wounds under the mantles

                         deep scars

hovering flies

over the immense well

stones want to rebel

the continent is shaken by the hatred and indifference

a wall of tradition and backwardness

grows inward and outward

the time of a world without violence looms in fear

walled screams shake the earth

robes and burkas flying over the city

a huge bonfire...

                         what doe not work is burned

sufferers of war, weapons, bestial men

                     fanatics, religions ...

horror does not want more horror

blood calls to blood

voices, choirs over the city

abyssal birds fly in circles

we have reached the limit

hands construct an escape staircase

without crushed Gods or millenarian cults

a light that blurs the red canvas

a light from the deep bowels of the earth.

CICATRICES

La mancha roja sobre la tierra negra crece sin control
miles de bocas gritan tras un velo negro
las heridas de la piel bajo los mantos
                         las cicatrices profundas
moscas revolotean sobre el inmenso pozo
las piedras quieren rebelarse
el continente se estremece ante el odio y la indiferencia
una muralla de tradición y atraso
                         crece hacia adentro y hacia fuera
el tiempo de un mundo sin violencia se asoma con miedo
gritos tapiados hacen temblar la tierra
mantos y burkas vuelan sobre la ciudad
una gran hoguera ilumina la noche
                         calcinado lo que no sirve
enfermos de guerra, armas, hombres bestiales
                         fanáticos, religiones…
el horror no quiere más horror
la sangre llama a la sangre
voces, coros sobre la ciudad
pájaros abismados vuelan en circulo
hemos llegado al limite
las manos construyen una escalera de fuga
sin dioses aplastantes, ni cultos milenarios
una luz que difumine el lienzo rojo

una luz desde las profundas entrañas de la tierra.

19 de Abril 2013

Alina Beatrice Chesca
Romania

Alina Beatrice Cheşcă was born on the 9th of June 1974 in the city of Constanţa, ROMANIA.

From October 1997 until now she has been a University Lecturer, with a PhD in English at "Danubius" University of Galaţi, Romania. From October 2009 through December 2010 she was a producer and presenter of the TV show "Learning in Europe" broadcast on the TV Galati channel.

In 2008 Alina earned her PhD in Philological Studies at "Ovidius" University of Constanța.

She has participated in about thirty international conferences, published numerous courses, and also papers in scientific magazines or in conference publications.

She is a member of the"Costache Negri" Writers' Society of Galați and an associate editor of two culture magazines.

Alina has published 7 poetry books: *The Girl with Waves-like Hair*, Evrika Publishing-House, Brăila; *Life with Every Breath*, Sinteze Publishing-House, Galați; *Fetița de la celălalt capăt de suflet/The Little Girl from the Other Side of the Soul*, Zigotto Publishing-House, Galați (released at Press Club, Calcutta, INDIA); *"The Odyssey Inside Us"* (cArtESENȚE Collection), "The Lower Danube" Cultural Centre Publishing-House, Galați; the bilingual poetry book „*Sărutul zeilor"/ Kiss of Gods*, Axis Libri Publishing-House, Galați; the bilingual poetry book *Jurnalul soarelui/Journal of the Sun*, Pax Aura Mundi Publishing-House, Galați; the children's book *"In the Garden of Spring"* (Ed. Zigotto, Galați) and the doctoral thesis *Mihail Sebastian – A Psychoanalytical Approach.*

She has published poems in more than ten culture magazines and is present in twelve poetry anthologies and books of literary criticism. She wrote eight forewords for poetry books and novels.

Alina received six poetry awards at national competitions and several diplomas for cultural contribution, and translated four poetry books into English and has three photographic exhibitions.

THE POETRY OF HAZARA

The wings are just

dreams taken to the sky of Hazara

learn one more time

that the world lies at poetry's feet

that mornings are poetry

nights are poetry

that love stories – the immense love stories

are just an endless poem

bigger than the world

and all universes together

music and dance

are also GOD's poetry

spread in air cells

through all skies of the world

may your wings take you

to the peace in Hazara

beyond yourselves

and beyond nowhere

it is still so much beauty in Hazara

it is not in vain that we are GOD's words

uttered in holy verses

DO NOT EVER LEARN HOW TO DIE

those who truly feel never learn it

they just create love stories beyond the body

they build pyramid-like words

stronger than time and death

flood the world with music of angels

DO NOT FORGET THAT EVERYTHING IS POETRY

EVEN IN HAZARA

LETTER TO GOD

GOD, put on my shoulders
the sadness of Hazara people
I am strong, GOD
I can turn the blood rivers into rainbows
on which all of us should go on a promenade
on Christmas, Ramadan, Hanukkah or Diwali

GOD, take my days and turn them into
clean blood for mortals
sap for woods and living water
for all creatures of the earth

take my poetry
and give it to those who want wars
convince them that the only war must be
the one for the supremacy of joy
take my air, GOD
and wrap up the Planet with flower scent
take my sight and
turn it into prayer rugs
take my food and sleep
and turn them into endless field and woods

GOD, I give you my memories as well
to make love stories greater than life

Alina Beatrice Chesca

take my books, but make the children of Hazara
live in an everlasting fairy-tale
take my friends and make them angels on Your right side
take my years and give the eternity to them, GOD
take my soul and divide it among seven billion people
but let everybody sing, dream and laugh
TAKE ALL I HAVE, ALL I KNOW, ALL I LOVE
AND GIVE PEOPLE
        ALL THEY CAN HAVE
            ALL THEY CAN KNOW
                AND ALL THEY CAN LOVE

Simón Zavala Guzmán
Ecuador

Poet, essayist, and jurist, Simon has published twenty books of poetry. Of these, five were with co-authors from Ecuador and Latin America. His books have been published in Ecuador, Argentina, Chile, Peru, Uruguay, and the United States of America.

Simón's works are in anthologies of important publications in Ecuador, Latin America, and Europe. He has given readings in Spain and several Latin American countries. Most of his poetry has been translated into English. Many of his poems have been translated into French, Italian, Portuguese, German, Arabic, and Hebrew.

FREEDOM FLOWER

Oh painful scar on the soul of the world!

Oh dreadful knife killing the heart of the world!

Oh damned death drinking the innocent blood of Hazara life!

Hazara tree people, resurrection people,

sky people full of star birds

You flourish between the death's malodorous jaws

murderers shall not annihilate you

assassins shall not bury you

assassins shall not overcome you

Flower people of immemorial times

Rose of eternity

Your voice is raised in every throat

of our humankind.

In the desert

in mountains

amid the winds and storms

in the clear waters kissing your body

naked in front of the avatars,

your ancestral spirits are sore

but strong

resisting death as immortal oaks

peacefully resisting the genocidal

traitors,

warmongers.

They will not win.

Over your heroic blood, Hazara,

death, sometime sooner

than later,

will have to stop

and you and your luminous people, filled with love,

will open their wings

to fly to the greatest human freedom.

FLOR DE LIBERTAD

Oh dolorosa cicatriz en el alma
del mundo
Oh terrible cuchilla matando el corazón
del mundo
Oh maldita muerte bebiendo la sangre
inocente de la vida Hazara.

Hazara pueblo árbol, pueblo resurrección,
pueblo cielo lleno de pájaros estrellas
creces entre las fauces malolientes de la
muerte
no te aniquilarán los asesinos
no te enterrarán los asesinos
no te vencerán los asesinos
pueblo flor de tiempo inmemorial
rosa de eternidad
tu voz se eleva en todas las gargantas
de nuestra humanidad.

En el desierto
en las montañas
en medio de los vientos y las tormentas
en las aguas cristalinas que besan tu cuerpo
desnudo frente a los avatares

están tus espíritus ancestrales adoloridos
pero fuertes
resistiendo a la muerte como robles
inmortales
resistiendo pacíficamente a los genocidas
a los traidores
a los guerreristas.

No te vencerán
sobre tu sangre heroica pueblo Hazara
la muerte, algún momento, más temprano
que tarde,
tendrá que detenerse
y tú y tu gente luminosa y llena de amor
abrirán sus alas
para volar a la más plena libertad humana.

Ostap Nozhak
Ukraine

Ostap Noshak was born on April 28, 1983 in Chortiv, Ukraine and currently lives in Chernivtsi, Ukraine. He graduated from M. Shashkevych Gymnasium and has an M.A. in Ukrainian Philology.

He worked as a reporter, proofreader, and artistic designer at the university newspaper from 2004 until 2007. Since 2006, he has taught classes in the journalism department of the same university while researching the history of publishing. He also teaches Polish. Ostap has won several poetry and language contests held in Chernivtsi and Kyiv and has been a participant in literary festivals. He has written one poetry collection, and contributed to collections of poetry, prose, and essays in literary magazines in the Ukraine, Poland, and Hungary. Noshak translates poetry and prose from Polish to Ukrainian and back again.

He also publishes a genealogy newspaper called *Zharynka*, or *Ember*.

HAZARA

and now I see a woman

yes I do see the woman

and she's Hazara I guess

yes she's Hazara for sure

her look is precise

like the rocks embracing her

her body is full of wind

her temples are full of sun

her hair is full of heat

her shadow is full of herself

that's she whom I see and hear

and feel and comprehend

well, the one who comprehends her the best

is her husband with whom she takes care

of her kids

as well as she is to do it

defending against destruction

and disappearance

for it wasn't a success with Buddha

what she has this power for – to take care

of her kids from enemies

i don't know

she doesn't as well

just takes care of them

with the shadow fulled by herself

ХАЗАРА

зараз я бачу жінку

так, я точно її бачу

вона, здається, Хазара

так вона Хазара точно

її погляд зіркий

як ці скелі навколо неї

її тіло наповнене вітром

її скроні наповнені сонцем

її волосся наповнене спекою

її тінь наповнена нею

таку її бачу і чую

і відчуваю і розумію

зрештою, найкраще її розуміє

її чоловік

з яким вона

як і належить

береже своїх дітей від знищення

і зникнення

бо Будду їй зберегти не вдалося

за що їй цей дар – берегти

своїх дітей від ворогів

не знаю

вона теж не знає

просто береже їх

тінню наповненою нею

Berry Heart
Botswana

Berry Heart, born Keotshepile Motseonageng, is a recording artist, poet, singer, dancer, and photographic model. Her first single album *Mama* was produced in Germany by Daniel Schmidt of Chabreteure Productions in 2008.

Berry holds a Bachelor's Degree in Arts (English Poetry), a certificate in German and is currently pursuing an International Diploma in French. In 2011 she produced an album entitled *Giving Birth to Love*. In 2012 she produced a charity poetry album, *Children of Mawa*, to raise funds for abused children. She is a member of the UN Creative Advisory Council.

Sometimes, Berry regards herself not as a poet but as an activist of intellectualized circumstance. She staged a live poetry performance at the Maharaja Conference Centre during the 16 Days Conference, where participants compiled poetry pieces based on the themes of the 16 days of activism to protest violence against women and children including abuse, rape, AIDS, and featuring the Universal Declaration of Human Rights.

Berry is a widely travelled poet who is the voice of the voiceless. She has staged shows in Africa and Europe. With Berry Heart, where there is a will there is a way.

A POEM FOR HAZARA PEOPLE

The height of my spiritual insight
grows as hearts throbbed
thoughts of innocent souls stained
my tearful eye finds no shape to cry
for the Hazara people

this poem speaks for the Hazara people
this poem builds a temple
to save a nation forbidden
wherefore hail thy hatred
for the Hazara people?

the pain makes my brain membranes insane

they said this is world of the free.

Gilma de los Ríos
Colombia

Gilma de los Rios was born in Manizales, Colombia.
She studied Social Communication and has been the director and editor of corporate publications and a university professor. She has been linked to projects of peace, human rights, and community development.

Gilma has written poetry since her youth and published two books: *Before the Silence**, published by the Rayo Museum in 1989 and *Recidivism*** in 1999, published by the Caldas Institute of Culture, and republished in Bogotá in 2000. This last one was published in Swedish, *Aterfall* for Annika Wiberg, edited by Simon Editor in 2001. Her poetry has been published in national and international anthologies.

Gilma has written several unpublished books of children's literature, and poetry such as *Meeting with the beautiful****, of which the published poem is a part.

* *Antes del Silencio*
** *Reincidencias*
*** *Encuentro con lo bello*

THE VIGIL

We awake.

The daily nightmare is extreme already.

How can we keep the heart still?

In an hibernation of skepticisms,

of easy escapes

and an unhealthy air of helplessness,

we dreamed on.

A desire of planetary love

still lived.

We awake.

We denounced the false boundaries

of homelands, geographies, religions and histories

and in one overwhelming "No!" to the hecatomb

we found the fraternal word once more

and a meaning to life.

Translation: Javier Zamudio

Gilma De Los Ríos

LA VIGILIA

Despertamos.
La pesadilla diaria ya es extrema.
¿Cómo dejar al corazón callado?

En una hibernación de escepticismos,
de fáciles escapes
y de un aire malsano de impotencias,
todavía soñábamos.

Aún vivía
un deseo de planetario amor.

Despertamos.
Desmentimos las supuestas barreras
de patrias, geografías, religiones e historias,
y en un no contundente a la hecatombe
encontramos de nuevo la palabra fraterna
y un sentido a la vida.

Del libro inédito: " Encuentro con lo bello"

Laura Hernandez Muñoz
México

Muñoz holds an undergraduate degree and an M.A. in History. She is a journalist and television and radio presenter as well as a poet, essayist, playwright and storyteller. She is a founder of the Institute of Cultural Development for Women and the founder of the Association of Children's Literature of Mexico. Her work has been published in numerous international magazines and books. She is the author of more than twenty books, the last seven dedicated to children and youth. The Children's Literature Association of Perú named the Fifth International Congress held in the city of Arequipa, in November 2011, the "Laura Hernández Muñoz Conference".

FAR FROM HEAVEN

there is a place on earth
where the gods give back
and look the other way.
Hazara is abandoned paradise Adam and Eve
place where flowers grow scented death
and Cain has returned to spread the pain
and steal the smiles of children.
Women no longer mourn their dead
because they have taken his eyes.
The left hate heartless men
that from a desk sign death sentences
unaware of his victims
for those are not important
Hazara refuses to die
because children still flourish
born of hope.

Mamang Dai
India

Mamang Dai was born in Pasighat, East Siang District, Arunachal Pradesh, and a native-born speaker of the Adi language. She is a poet and novelist who writes in English. She was a correspondent for *The Hindustan Times*, *The Telegraph*, and *The Sentinel* newspapers, and is the President of the Arunachal Pradesh Union of working journalists. Mamang also worked with World Wide Fund for Nature in the Eastern Himalaya Biodiversity Hotspots program.

Mamang has been featured in several national and international forums to promote the disappearing traditions of her state in the face of modernity and give voice to its people through the imaginative space of prose and poetry.

Dai is a long time member of the North East Writers' Forum (NEWF) and recipient of the Padma Shri, 2011, for Literature and Education.

Currently she is a Member of the Arunachal Pradesh Public Service Commission.

Dai lives in Itanagar, Arunachal Pradesh, India.

From my village
the land of strangers is very far away.
There is no road to travel there.
I fly with the birds.

A hawk spreads its wings.

When the winter wind
comes howling down the gorge
seeds of bitterness swirl in the air.
A cloud breaks my heart.

It rains.
The red mountain is weeping.
There is war, and there is death,
but the birds painted blue and gold are flying on
escorting wandering souls

Over the frozen valley,
beyond the thin peaks,
the air is full of promise.
A strange light draws my eyes
intense, with signs of life.

The clouds are breaking open.
A shining ridge tilts towards the sun.

Erkut Tokman
Turkey

Erkut Tokman is a Turkish poet, actor, visual artist, and translator who was born in İstanbul in 1971. He studied poetry, modern dance and acting in London, Bucharest, and Milan. He has published his poems, poetry translations, articles, and several stories in leading Turkish literary magazines since 1996.

Erkut's poetry books are *Giden ve Kalan*-1999-Liman yapımevi (Arrivals and departures from Soul-Liman Publishing House), and

Bilinmezi Dolaşan Ses-2007-Yitik Ülke yayınları (Strolling voice of eternity-Yitik Ülke Publishing house.) He is a member of the Poets of London, Poetas Del Mondo, Intercultural Translation Academy of Turkey, and Turkish P.E.N- Member of WinP (Writers in Prison Committee).

Erkut is a founding member of "The House of Wisdom" (Granada-Spain) and a Board member of EDISAM (Turkish literature and science publishers association). His poems have been translated into different languages and published abroad.

I REMEMBER WHAT MEANS HAZARA

I remember what means freedom
When once you were there to give a birth
to the most beautiful people of Hazara
Breeding dignity of one nation I was: Now named
Under genocide struggling against oppression

I remember what means Hazara once
Those lands of freedom
Carried away my death body
which were in bits and pieces under blast
Yet I am still here you may not see
Next to you by my soul in struggle and trust

I remember what means to be alive once
They say deaths still can live among us
Thus the livings for those who are in silent are alike

I remember what means solidarity
When one cures our sorrowful existence
Here or there on earth you will see discrimination
Racism, aberration and the others
I remember what was meant Humanity once
We were like brothers!

HATIRLIYORUM HAZARA NE ANLAMA GELIR

Hatırlıyorum özgürlük ne demektir
Bir zamanlar sende ordaydın
Dünyanın en güzel Hazara insanlarına yaşam vermek için
Bir ulusun çoğalan onuruydum. Şimdiyse adım
Baskıya direnen soykırım

Hatırlıyorum Hazara ne demektir
Şu özgürlüğün toprağı
Benim ölü vücudumu taşıdı
Patlamaların altında parçalara bölünmüş
Ama ben hala buradayım göremeyebilirsin
Senin yanında direnen ve inançlı ruhumla

Hatırlıyorum bir zamanlar canlı olmak nedir
Derlerki ölüler hala yaşarlar
Oysa yaşayanlar ki sessizlik içinde,onlarda aynılar

Hatırlıyorum dayanışma ne demektir
Biri bizim acılı varlığımızı iyileştirdiğinde
Burda yada orda göreceksin ayrımcılığı
Irkçılığı, sapkınlığı ve diğerlerini
Hatırlıyorum bir zamanlar insanlık ne demekti
Bizler kardeş gibiyken!

                                              11/14.06.2013-Istanbul

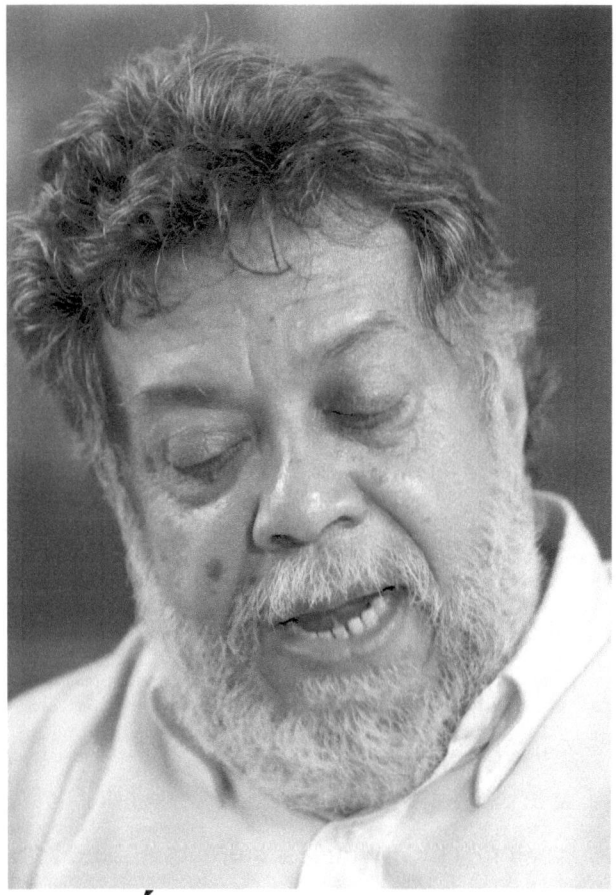

Álvaro Miranda
Colombia

Álvaro Miranda is a poet and novelist born in Colombia and is the author of the following books: *Los escritos de don Sancho Jimeno, Simulación de un reino,* and *La última épica del Cid.*

His novel *La risa del cuervo* was awarded the Premio Nacional de Novela from Instituto de Cultura de Colombia. With sponsored recognition for Latin American writers he was granted a residence to write his third novel *Muchachas como nubes*, after having published *Un cadáver para armar* and other books, the most prominent of which is *Crónicas para olvidar la historia y Jorge Eliécer Gaitán el fuego de una vida.*

A MOON FOR THE HAZARAS

On the carriage of the night -so I call my house when it is darkening and the sky dinner the sun's rays, I see death obscure threads running through the bodies of the living; women who, in the light of their oil lamps illuminate the moon that is repeated on the ponds, the elderly who drink a drop of water off the hook of a ghost of mist; widows collecting the words that lead the ears to the wind; murmuring blind alligators in the sewers of an abandoned village; ant skin resting on Bamiyan Buddha's dust, the gardens of Babylon that perfume a silent dead. On the carriage the day-so I call my house at dawn, I see women who scare the trotting unicorn over snow transparencies, girls who pack a spark of star in the vegetable market of Quetta, the teenager girl who cries over wingless shirts that fade from blood, the fiery tears that smeared lightning flashes over the plains of the earth.

UNA LUNA PARA LOS HAZARAS

Sobre el carro de la noche- así llamo a mi casa cuando oscurece y el cielo cena los rayos del sol-, veo los hilos oscuros de la muerte que atraviesan los cuerpos de los vivos; las mujeres que, bajo la luz de sus lámparas de aceite, alumbran la luna que se repite en las charcas; los ancianos que beben un gota de agua descolgada de un fantasma de niebla; las viudas que recogen las palabras que llevan las espigas al viento; los cocodrilos ciegos que murmuran en las alcantarillas de un pueblo abandonado; la piel de las hormigas que reposan sobre el polvo del Buda de Bamiyan; los jardines de Babilonia que aroman un muerto silencioso.

Sobre el carro del día- así llamo a mi casa cuando amanece, veo las mujeres que espantan al unicornio que trota sobre las transparencias de la nieve, las niñas que empacan una chispa de estrella en el mercado de verduras de Quetta, la adolescente que llora sobre las camisas sin alas de los que palidecen sin sangre, la ígnea lágrima que embadurnó la luz de los relámpagos sobre las planicies de la tierra.

Claus Ankersen
Denmark

Claus Ankersen (b. 1123 and 1986).

Claus is an intergalactic traveler working with multiple artistic expressions, including live-literature and performance poetry. Claus Ankersen has been instrumental in the development of Danish spoken word, and has inscribed the genre in literary history with his documentary 'Peanuts and Free Beer' (2009).

He has exhibited museum installations, exorcised demons for National Danish Broadcast TV (DR), made a surreal spoken word show of butter at SMK (Danish State Museum of Art), and created himself in vivo in the word on stages all over Denmark for more than a decade.

Besides four books of poetry and a poetry, CD Ankersen has contributed to numerous anthologies in Denmark as well as internationally. His latest publications include contributions to the American anthology *Have a NYC – New York Short Stories*, and a new Danish release from December 2010, called *The Tree and The Fountain*, recently given four stars and termed 'Hipster poetry of the First Class', by Danish newspaper *Ekstrabladet*. The book is currently in pipeline for publication in India.

Internationally Claus Ankersen has performed, worked, and exhibited in Denmark, Sweden, Norway, Iceland, Finland, Estonia, Ukraine, Germany, Poland, Holland, Serbia, Croatia, Turkey, Armenia, India, and the USA. He has done readings at various literature- and art festivals, and guest- lectured on performance poetry and poetics at various universities and academic conferences. He was recently appointed vice-member of the board of the Finnish poetry organization Poetryweek.

Claus' poems have been translated into Swedish, Finnish, Polish, Ukrainian, and English, with Hindi and Malayalam translations pending. In April 2013, the artist installed a stele of letters 'ALWAYS' perhaps the largest poem in the world on a major Copenhagen Square. In June of 2013, he published a cross-disciplinary, bilingual collection, *Souvenirs from Heaven*.

VOICE OF THE VOICELESS

Voice of The Voiceless

Void in a null

sum of skin, bone, skull, blood

and sex

Voice of The Witless

hovering through air nobody breathes

save from sunlight

Exit anonymity

    Exit incognito

Enter the seventh seal and the blood of the lamb

on the meek

the numb, deaf and dumb

The toothless smile of a homeless

The soulless smile

of a clerk, or a toothpaste salesman

Death to them all as they toothpaste the whole world

The Fish, the Trees

    The little children of Africa – The persecuted tribes of the world

The dying languages

The forgotten codes

all covered in toothpaste and Martian vision; a smile for a coke

or a flat screen TV; a flat screen TV for a flat globe.

Hello Mister pancake, smeared on long-legged do-good automatons
shark-toothed, tooth-paste reptilian-hearted
The Voice
of the voiceless roaming thru:

    "Make me a rock star! Fashion me in your image", barren God of ambition,

greedy worm, piss ant lord of empty rhetoric's and dull minds.

    Put an iron crown on my forehead and let me forever leave myself and

become human – sitting behind the old me in a theater, hidden by darkness and shining love.

The Voice of the voiceless, devouring the Old
Toothpaste salesmen dangling from city lampposts, Gazprom moguls dead in their own puke,
Industry closed, chimneys cold
but grass my friend
    grass green, eyes radiating, live loving

We will shed the skin of glittering illusion and dance with the satyrs under a moon
where no one is lonely, empty, sad or sick.
And be thou ware, Mister toothpaste seller
Not only shells are legion.

Say not the holiest of holiest; We the Gods are The Voice of The Voiceless

Faceless we are, anonymous we are, all the things you fear are we.

Under a harvest moon, crimson from the big cleansing, we shall prevail

We sleep not in death and earth spins our way

Hail The Voice of The Voiceless. Come such we crown the kingdom and SHINE.

Mark Lipman
USA

Mark Lipman, a writer, poet, multi-media artist, and activist, began his career as a professional ballet dancer. In 2002, he became the writer-in-residence at Shakespeare and Company in Paris, under the guidance of its founder George Whitman. In that year he worked with Lawrence Ferlinghetti, Jack Hirschman and the Italian poet, Igor Costanzo, in *Back to Beat*, a Fluxus art and poetry event in Breccia, Italy.

Co-founder of the *Berkeley Stop the War Coalition* (USA), *Agir Contre la Guerre* (France) and *Occupy Los Angeles*, he has been an outspoken critic of war and occupation since 2001.

Mark's works include: sixty original paintings; the novels *Impermanence* (2001); *Fire in the Desert* (2003); *Tumbleweed* (2004); *A Smuggler's Tale* (2006); and several books of poetry including *Because They Were Happy and Free* (Caza de Poesía, 2009); *The Dirt of Despair* (Caza de Poesía, 2010) and *A Stirring Underfoot* (Caza de Poesía, 2011), and most recently a collection of his economic essays, *Global Economic Amnesty* (Vagabond, 2013). He is also a member of the Revolutionary Poets Brigade (RPB). His website is www.vagabondbooks.net

THOUSAND

A thousand years go by too fast
  for the children of Khan
  for the children of the fields and land.

The sounds of Bonsai and Hazara
  echo from the past
  recalling simpler days
  before the king's horsemen
  before the rifles of the emir
  would decide who had the right to be human.

A thousand years go by
  in the flash of an eye
  and the hint of cyanide
  surrounds the almond tree
  forewarning our greatest struggle
  the bitter seed of time
  the progress that marches over our existence
  stealing our land, taxing our lives with blood and debt.

If a thousand years has taught us anything
  it's that all the advancements
  are first put into the hands of the oppressor
  to divide the poor and weak
  to pit our tribes against each other,

while some banker, half a world away

lives in splendor, laughing at our feuds and fate.

It's not the ragged shoes

or unwashed faces

that is cause for our suffering

but the blatant disregard

for our humanity

of our right to self determination.

For a thousand years we built

our temples, our culture and traditions

then one day an airplane flew over our heads

draped in a colonial flag

and bombed us into the stone age.

A thousand years go by

having seen so much

and learned so little.

What will they say in the next millennium?

Will our children still have a place to live

in a thousand years from now?

Will they long for the piece of dirt we hold today?

What world do we leave for those yet to be born?

Can we see a thousand years down the line?

Hazara – Hazara

A thousand years,
　how quickly it goes by.

Hazara, translated from the Persian, means 'thousand'.
Cyanide, a derivative from bitter almonds. Almond trees being an economic staple of the Hazara region of Nili, in Dai Kundi, Afghanistan.

WHO'S YOUR HERO?

Someone who we all know to be lying,
or someone who tells the truth?

Someone who hides behind the draping of power to do what is wrong,
or someone who puts his life on the line to do what is right?

Someone who blatantly disregards the constitution for the sake of expediency,
or someone who fulfills the oath they have taken?

These are questions we must ask ourselves.

Should we trust someone who puts their faith in secrecy,
or someone who brings forth transparency?

Someone who distrusts and spies on his own citizenry,
or someone who exposes the lies for the sake of his country?

Should we be challenging the one who blew the whistle,
or the one who committed the crime in the first place?

You decide what you want to believe,
as for me, I side with the latter.

John Hegley
England

John Hegley, born 1953, is an English poet and singer whose father was a native of France. He has performed in Zanzibar, Portugal, India and Columbia, where the event was held in a womens' prison. He lives with his partner and cat.

I OBSERVE THE LIST OF HAZARA PROVERBS

I observe the list of Hazara proverbs

untranslated

and not understood by me.

And yet I know that within these other wisdoms

there will be recognition of patterns true to my own trail of experience.

A common ground

to be found in the future, I hope.

The list is long.

Here's to the common ground.

Here's to the tread of Hazara people,

untrembling

untroubled,

strong

and understood.

I'm wondering what those Hazara proverbs might have to say.

The riverbed in drought provides a pathway?

The mountaingoat is not a social climber

The eucalyptus shades without exception?

A multitude of minds can move a mountain?

Micere Githae Mugo
Kenya

Micere Githae Mugo (born Madeleine Mugo in 1942) is a playwright, author, activist, instructor, and poet from Kenya. She is a literary critic and professor of literature in the Department of African American Studies at Syracuse University.

She was forced into exile in 1982 from Kenya during the Daniel Arap Moi dictatorship for activism and moved to teach in Zimbabwe, and later the United States. Mwalimu Mugo teaches Orature,

Literature, and Creative Writing. Mugo's publications include six books, a play co-authored with Ngũgĩ wa Thiong'o and three monographs. She has also edited journals and the Zimbabwean school curriculum. The East African Standard Century listed her among the most influential people in Kenya in 2002 – "The Top 100: They influenced Kenya Most during the 20th century". (Wikipedia)

HAZARA PEOPLE AND HISTORY LIVE ON!

Unending war condemns Hazara homesteads into graveyards
Trampling boots stomp the soft earth, turning it into hard stone
Angry guns spit out venom, silencing children, women and men
Bodies of generations of the Hazara litter the land of their birth
But from under these historical genocide sites their ancestors rise
Summoning the dead to life; breathing new life into the living-dead
Reminding them that no flood, however powerful, can ever bury
The history of a people
Counseling them that no tsunami, however violent, can ever drown
The life force of a culture
Consoling them that no chains, however strong, can ever shackle
The soul of a people

Declaring, with the poets of the world,
That Hazara people and history live on!

Germain Droogenbroodt
Belgium/Spain

Germain Droogenbroodt is a poet and translator of poetry, born in Belgium, but living in Spain. He has written eleven, and translated over thirty poetry books.

Germain is the founder-editor of POINT which published eighty books of international poetry, and is also president of the Spanish Cultural Foundation ITHACA. His mystical, philosophical poetry is a poetic bridge between Eastern and Western cultures and has been published in twenty-four countries. Germain Droogenbroodt has been invited to the world's most prestigious international poetry festivals. He has received several poetry awards and an honorary doctorate for his literary activities.

FUGE OF DEATH (ANNO 2013)

*Variation on the famous poem by Paul Celan,
dedicated to the Hazara people*

Dark blood of the morning
   dark blood of the day

  dark blood of the evening

  dark blood of the night

we drink it, we drink and we drink

dark blood of your children

dark blood of your women

dark blood of your men

we drink it, we drink and we drink

we drink it, we drink it every day.

but, *haben wir es gewußt?*

yes, we did!

* the poem is a reference to the famous poem "Todesfuge" by Paul Celan about the smoke of the German gas chambers in which millions of Jews were exterminated during World War II. After the war, Germans pretended that they did not know about the holocaust (wir haben es nicht gewußt). But did they really not know it? We know about present killings and exterminations, but what do we do?

PEACEFUL MORNING IN THE HIMALAYAS

It appears
as if the previous night
has quenched every thirst

the day comes with light
and voices of birds
strange to the ear

in the distance
the wavering sound
of a reed flute:

a morning prayer
for Shiva, for Buddha
or for whatever god

so peaceful appears this morning
as if after so many ages
humanity were at peace
finally at rest.

From: "In the Stream of Time, Meditations in the Himalayas"

Germain Droogenbroodt

Fiyinfoluwa Onarinde
Nigeria

Born at Ilesa, Osun State over two decades ago, Onarinde Fiyinfoluwa has paraded his poetic ingenuity to bring to the foreground the reminiscences of the past into the present.

This inchoate urge was drummed in his first anthology entitled: *BIRTH OF AN AFRICAN POET*, in which his passion and unalloyed adoration is given to the African Culture. His Admiration for Africanism and the recent upsurge all over the African Continent and beyond of democratic forces also pervades through his poetry.

Onarinde has been published in several international journals. He contributed to the *World Peace World Healing* poetry collection published by Inner Child Press based in the USA. He has performed in different literary national poetry events including the International Conference of Students of the English Language in Nigeria.

The poet is a member of the Association of Nigerian authors, the Writehouse Collective, HIVOS, Africalia, Puma Creative Africa, ARTerial; a joint founder of the PacessterPoets and the founder of AfriqueArts a non-governmental organization that explores the versatility of the arts to campaign against AIDS and raise funds to provide jobs for unemployed youths in Nigeria.

Suffice it to say that his academic cum-experience has spurred him to writing a series of literary works, and journals. Onarinde is currently a graduate student of Literature of the Department of English, University of Ibadan, Nigeria.

LONG BEFORE THE GATHERING TWILIGHT...

There was an abode consecrated with graceful smiles

Long before we become a simile for pain

An allegory for slavery

Before this whirling tempest

Dispersed us like pollens of the tridax

Blowing off the grand-stand of peace,

We gathered in blissful camaraderie

In a boogie of banquets

Now when the dancers are feasted on

In the rage of furious neighbors

Who with their guns arbitrate in the carnival of death?

 Lauded by the devil's advocates.

Of bombs and mines

Our serene home drifts

In this shave with desolations breathe.

Will the earth sing her song?

Will she gather her son's home?

Like a dispersed flock to their barn,

While she chants her canticle of nurture

Let her sing

Tell her not to wail

Sing! Sing! Sing!

Mother Sing!

That Hazara may feast again on these peaks.

Ataol Behramoğlu
Turkey

Ataol Behramoglu (Turkey) is a significant poet and peacemaker from Turkey who has published over twenty books of poetry. In March of 1982, he was arrested along with other executive committee members of the Turkish Peace Association and kept under atrocious conditions in Maltepe Military Prison until he was conditionally released in November of 1982. He was awarded the Lotus Prize by the Afro Writers Union in 1982.

In November 1983, at the Turkish Peace Association Trial, Behramoglu was sentenced to eight years of hard labor followed by three years of exile. He had to leave his country and in 1984, went to Paris to participate in the work of the Sorbonne's National Institute for Oriental Languages and Civilizations, Center for Comparative Poetry.

Atatol's poems have been widely translated and published in several languages. In 1985, he was awarded an M.A. degree (Diplômes D'études Approfondies/D.E.A) by the Center for Comparative Poetry for his study on the poetry of Nazım Hikmet and Vladimir Mayakovsky. The same year in Germany, his two new books of poetry were published in Turkish: *Turkey, My Sad Country, My Beautiful Land,* and *Letters to My Daughter.*

In 2003, he was awarded The Great Prize of Poetry by the Turkish International P.E.N. Besides his widespread popularity as a poet and writer in his country, he is an eminent translator of the works of Russian poets and writers such as Pouchkine, Lermontov, Chekov, and Gorky. Ataol Behramoğlu is currently the head of the Russian Philology Department in İstanbul-Aydın University and also writes a column as a literary and political commentator in the daily Cumhuriyet.

BABIES DON'T HAVE NATIONS

Babies don't have nations
I felt this for the first time far from my homeland
Babies don't have nations
The way they hold their heads is the same
They gaze with the same curiosity in their eyes
When they cry, the tone of their voices is the same

Babies are the blossoms of humankind
Of roses the most pure, most the buds of roses
Some are fair fragments of light
Some are dusky-dark grapes

Fathers, do not let them slip your minds
Mothers, protect your babies
Silence them, silence them, don't let them speak
Who would talk of war and destruction

Let us leave them to grow up with passion
May they sprout and burgeon like saplings
They are not yours, nor mine, nor anybody's
They belong to the whole world
They are the apple of all humanity's eye

I felt this for the first time far from my homeland
Babies don't have nations

Babies are the blossoms of humankind

And our future's one tiny hope

Translation: Walter G. Andrews

BEBEKLERİN ULUSU YOK

İlk kez yurdumdan uzakta yaşadım bu duyguyu
Bebeklerin ulusu yok
Başlarını tutuşları aynı
Bakarken gözlerinde aynı merak
Ağlarken aynı seslerin tonu

Bebekler çiçeği insanlığımızın
Güllerin en hası, en goncası
Sarışın bir ışık parçası kimi
Kimi kapkara üzüm tanesi

Babalar çıkarmayın onları akıldan
Analar koruyun bebeklerinizi
Susturun susturun söyletmeyin
Savaştan yıkımdan söz ederse biri

Bırakalım sevdayla büyüsünler
Serpilip gelişsinler fidan gibi
Senin benim hiç kimsenin değil
Bütün bir yeryüzünündür onlar
Bütün insanlığın gözbebeği

lk kez yurdumdan uzakta yaşadım bu duyguyu
Bebeklerin ulusu yok

Bebekler, çiçeği insanlığımızın
               Ve geleceğimizin biricik umudu...

Khal Torabully
Mauritius/France

Khal Torabully was born in Mauritius and studied Semiology of Poetics (PhD) in Lyon, France. He has published twenty poetry books and been included in various anthologies and participated in several festivals.

Khal devised the poetics of *coolitude*, a humanism of diversity inspired by indentured migrations, now studied in many countries. He is a member of POINTS, (transearea studies) in Berlin and founder of the House of Wisdom, in Granada, Spain. He is regarded as a major poet of the Indian Ocean. Torabully has won awards for his poetry and films in France, the UK, Egypt, and Switzerland.

SOUL OF HAZARAS

For the downtrodden

between the Hindu Kouch

and the crimson clouds,

burdens of shadows

reach the peaks of oblivion.

Some say they were Mongols and soldiers,

some gave them insults and blows.

Others bought them for some shillings,

but behold, these people know the weight of mountains

and the lightness of a sudden rain!

Hazaras have met the eagle

and talked to the crows.

In those forlorn valleys, many know

how their looks have reconciled

the pangs of emptiness

with the desires of immortality.

For, never in vain,

does a child flying a kite dream !

July 2013

Jorge Boccanera
Argentina

Poet, Playwright and Essayist Jorge Boccanera was born in Bahía Blanca, Buenos Aires in 1952. He has lived in exile for several years in Mexico and Central America. In 1976, he won the prize "Casa de las Americas" in Cuba, and later the "National Award for Young Poets" in Mexico. In 2008, he won VIII Premio Casa de América de Poesía Americana for his book, *Palma real*.

NAZIM HIKMET'S EYES SPEAK

In my hand,
Half an apple shines.
The other half lies on a table thousands of
Kilometers from here.

It's impossible to bite this half
without the emptiness hurting.

HABLAN LOS OJOS DE NAZIM HIKMET

Sobre mi mano,

la mitad de una manzana brilla.

La otra mitad está sobre una mesa a miles de

   kilómetros de aquí.

Es imposible morder esta mitad

sin que duela el vacío.

KAMANDA Kama Sywor
Congo

KAMANDA Kama Sywor was born in Luebo, Congo in 1952. This writer's poetry, novels, and folk-tales illustrate the dual influences of Ancient Egypt, his Ancestors' Land, and of his rich Bantu ancestry.

Ten collections of poetry, in which the celebration of Africa and the anguish of exile and solitude are recurring themes, have earned him international recognition. Kamanda's work has been widely translated and appears in international literary journals. His numerous literary awards include:

Prix Paul Verlaine de l'Académie Française, 1987
Prix Louise Labé, 1990
Grand Prix littéraire de l'Afrique noire, 1991
Prix Théophile Gautier de l'Académie Française, 1993
Prix Mélina Mercouri de l'Association des poètes et écrivains grecs, 1999.

Poet of the Millennium-2000 Award - International Poets Academy (India)
Citoyen d'honneur de Joal-Fadiouth (Sénégal), 2000.
Prix de poésie de la Société internationale des écrivains grecs, 2002.
Top 100 Writers, 2005, International Biographical Centre
Certificat d'honneur Maurice Cagnon, CIEF, 2005
Special Literary Award, CIEF, 2005
Professional of the year 2005, IBC, (United Kingdom), 2005
Man of the year 2005, ABI (United States)
International Peace Prize 2006, United Cultural Convention
Prix Heredia de l'Académie Française (Œuvre poétique), 2009

ATONEMENT

On the beach of pearls

The waves beat each other.

Under a sky livid in its immobility,

The moon in the sphere of love

Stares at the architect of our dreams.

Oh Creator of lives, time set adrift

Takes the winds out of our sails of miracles

And the obstacles clashed by thought,

Carries along the winds of our silent memories.

Ghosts in the high grasses

Work the imprints of our dead

Now forgotten.

Thus, in the night of the storytellers,

The tales bear the same message

As the elegies of our ancestors, gods and spirits.

Expiation
Kama Sywor KAMANDA
in *"L'étreinte des mots"*
Translated by Jane Kostas

THE BLOOD OF SILENCES

Mask your thoughts before my suns,

Your passions before my limitless excesses

Be the prophet of my distant shores,

Oracle of my indomitable seasons of love

Where ecstasies bin themselves to the void.

The immortal flame comes to rest upon you

And yet I dream still of roots

Anchored to the legends of the zebra sky dreams

Like the flash of lightning.

The light of eternities

Cradles your spheres behind the dawn

Tormented that it cannot feed my hopes

And teach me of your amorous designs.

When your body ignites in the heat

My pleasures find in you their tomb.

O promise stripped bare !

Caress my desire for embers.

I enfold in an illusion the blood of silences.

Les silences d'un fantôme
Kama Sywor KAMANDA
in *"L'étreinte des mots"*
Translated by Andrew Evans

BITTERNESS

In my memory remain the ashes of my transfigured loves.

Dawn penetrates me like a warm rain

On old remembrances and torments.

I freed my vision of the symbols

And vestiges of the past; but forgot

To purge history of its characters.

The departing twilight takes with it

Neither my sorrows nor my regrets.

Hardly can I prevent the tumults of the pallid horizons.

Storms have ravaged my soul

And the drought has dried up my passion.

My pain is old.

Will I once again dream of a new flame

To rock the ultimate consciousness ?

Sad face with tangled wrinkles,

It is no longer possible for me to be mistaken.

From now on, I will chant only

The complaints of my still life in exile

Filled with languor.

Amertume
Kama Sywor KAMANDA
in *"L'exil des songes"*
Translated by Jane Kostas

INTIMATE EXCERPT

In the tombs of my loves

I decompose the pride of time,

The anguish of my life

And the plots of the world.

I question eternity and death

On the ambiguity of being.

I walk towards the shores of the future

And cross fate's infinity.

Your dreams are extinguished discreetly

In the inviolate night of my closed aura.

Bliss sheltered from twilights,

Fled in the greedy dust,

Here am I in the depths of the past,

Penetrating the walls of destiny.

I take along my doubts and my sorrows

Like the sea all its effluvia.

Extrait intime
Kama Sywor KAMANDA
in *"L'exil des songes"*
Translated by Jane Kostas

FROM THE BEYOND

From the beyond come back often

The voices of our dead.

But what must we say about birds who dream

To heal the wounds of our inner hearts ?

Faith suspended in the transfiguration of the real,

Weaves stars in our dreams.

Oh! The awakening of the sky,

I lit the word under the ashes.

In the flesh of sacrifices,

Life inscribes its aspirations

And underwrites its loans to the dead.

May one spread over the sands of the homeland,

The patterns of language adrift.

The flood seasons always compose

The same refrain for our poems.

De l'au-delà
Kama Sywor KAMANDA
in *"Les vents de l'épreuve"*
Translated by Jane Kostas

PROPHECY

I tremble to the profound song of vanishing destiny.

In the whirlwind of dreams I cling

To the desire of a woman absent

And moving in myself I feel

All the tumult of love.

I pass where blood ploughs the river of life

Seeking in the countless faces yet unborn

Remembrance dedicated to this unfulfilled desire

To be united only in the dust.

I murmur to the wind of resurrection

My migrant's prophecy

As I progress through the mortal remains,

The injuries and the rumors.

And yet from the depth of my ancestral roots

I invite you, companion of my dreams,

To keep watch over my promised eternity,

Mingling your blood with mine

Where the world ends on blossoming

Prophétie
Kama Sywor KAMANDA
in *"Les vents de l'épreuve"*
Translated by Andrew Evans

Bineesh Puthuppanam
India

Bineesh Puthuppanam was born at Caliut, Kerala, in India. He has a degree in Education and a Graduate degree in Sanskrit. He participated in many national and international poetry festivals and has published many poems, critiques, and articles in the Malayalam language. His notable works are *The Drawbacks of Kerala Renaissance*, *Knowledge Construction*, *The Sea and the Moon Light*, and *The Poem in Pandanus Tree*.

Bineesh has his own interpretation in Bhajagovinda, a Sanskrit philosophical work of the Sankaracharya. Presently he is doing research in Sanskrit at Sree Sankaracharya University of Kalady.

WITHIN……..

Shirt

If the button is broken

It is torn

If worn it turned

easily noticed

because that is shirt

Trousers,

If it is shade

If zip is broken

If it is tattered

Noticed easily

Because

That is trousers

But

Inward what…?

If torn ……. Tattered

If wet

Who knows one's inward

Without

And who knows

One's heart.

Iris Miranda
Puerto Rico

Iris Miranda was born in Santurce, Puerto Rico in 1961. At an early age, her grandmother discovered her first written poem and celebrated it and all the following poems until her death.

Iris obtained BA and MA degrees in Hispanic Studies from the University of Puerto Rico. She has worked as a proofreader and workshop speaker, giving lectures on the subjects of university education and poetry. She collaborates with the International Poetry Festival in Puerto Rico and has coordinated several literary contests. She is currently part of the Faculty of the Polytechnic University of Puerto Rico in Hato Rey.

Mrs. Miranda belongs to the poets of the Generation of 1980, and her works have been published in electronic journals such as *En la orilla.net, Isla Negra, Sequoyah Virtual, Delirium Tremens, En sentido figurado.com*, among others. She has two books published currently, and two more on the way: *Noches de luna: embelesos y melismas (Orbis, 2007)* and *Alcoba Roja (La Iguana, 2011)*.

THE POWER OF A POEM

I travel all around the world,
looking for the gift the assassins had lost
Then, little flowers pointed out a center
leading, to a cave, my hope.

I could not see the heart of the murderers
I could not see their consciousness.
They have bartered them
for hate and torture…
Their kindness flew away
and, sadly, did I from the cave.
But a timid shadow stopped me
held my skirt to say:
I am the last gift they left inside
That is why they are so cruel
I am their remorse, their regret
So their eyes turned blind,
so their hands turned red.
But a powerful poem is weaving wires
to restore their lost hearts,
their clouded consciousness,
their forgotten kindness,
their remorse and their regret

Iris Miranda

Pamela Ateka
Kenya

Pamela Ateka is the author of the poetry book, *Sing Africa Sing*. In 2009 she represented Kenya and Africa in the sixth global Poetry Festival in Caracas, Venezuela. She is the founder of the Nairobi International Poetry Festival and hosted its first international festival in Kenya in 2005.

She presented a paper on "The Imagination of Poetry in the HIV/Aids Pandemic" in Stirling, hosted by the University of Stirling in Scotland. Pamela is well-traveled, and has performed and read poetry in many world forums. Pamela is the founder of Community Focus Group (CFG) and the chairperson and founder of Women in Democracy and Governance (WIDAG)-Kenya.

"We were all made"
in his image
in his image
we were all made
black, red, white, green
one love
one heart
one blood
we are
Humankind

Fahredin Shehu
Kosovo

Fahredin Shehu was born in Rahovec, in the south east of Kosova, in 1972. He graduated from Prishtina University, with a degree in Oriental Studies.

His published books include:
Nun, collection of mystical poems, *Invisible Plurality*- Poetical prose, *Nektarina*- novel/transcendental epic, *Elemental 99*- collection of transcendental lyrics, *Logos-A* and *Dismantle of Hate*- e-books, *Crystalline Echoes*- Poetry, *Plemora's Dew* and *Mulberries*- novels.

Shehu is the Ambassador of Poets to Albania by Poetas del Mundo, Santiago de Chile, and a member of the World Poets Association, Kosovo Pen Center.

O HUMAN

If we would compete in goodness as we do in evil
Today Angels would serve us with the Elixir
In Diamond goblets on crystalline tray

…for Human that never ponder on Humanity

The Poet has a say: the original Word that bursts

As ripe pomegranate-The outer Peace within the internal-

Infernal self- whirlpool of tormenting collective bleeding

In every corner of the World

And the Poet "I"- suffers for the wounds throughout

As part of the same entire body of the World, it suffered,

It suffers It'll suffer- Corresponding malice and ignorance…

And later I realize

Why Angels and Demons have mocked Human…

"Why these are killing each other?"

April 2013

Tamer Öncul
Cyprus

Tamer Öncul was born on October 3, 1960 in Nicosia. He graduated from the Dentistry Faculty of İstanbul University in 1984. He worked in İstanbul until 1990 and currently works as a dentist in Cyprus. He started writing poetry in the 1970s, searching for a new style, mixing realism with a sensitivity to "Cypriotness."

Tamer was instrumental in establishing the Turkish Cypriot Artists and Writers Association between 1992 and 1996, and has been its head ever since. He is also one of the founders of the magazine *Pygmalion*, which was first published in 1993.

Tamer's poetry has appeared in magazines in Turkey, Germany and France, as well as his native Cyprus, and his works have been

translated in to English, Greek, Bulgarian, German, Lithuanian, Ukrainian, and French.
They have also found their way into various anthologies.

He won the Cyprus Turkish Peace Association Poetry and Peace Price in 1982.

."You Ask Me, / Why do you write so much /about war, poet. / To disgust you who are at war..."

Poetry Books
The Diary of the Child who Lost His Days -İstanbul, 1987
The World is a Poem –Lefkoşa, 1992
I Hora –The City- Lefkoşa, 1996
The Street of Lost Loves- Lefkoşa, 1996
Dreams of Daytime –İstanbul, 1998
Inscriptions of Dried Spring –Lefkoşa, 2003

Other Books
Activites of Cyprus-Turkish Youths in Higher Education – Research and Eclectic-Lefkoşa, 1999 (written with Öntaç Düzgün)
Toyki- Eclectic, Lefkoşa, 2003

SMOKEY EARTH

With tulle wings
The mist caressed the moon
And knelt in front.

The night is howling
Wrapped in balding fur.
A faint shiver, on cold skin.

The earth exhaled smoke, slowly
Like warm soup on boil
A faint ache, on swollen groin.

The old door with broken knocker
Has tired, creaky hinges
The key don't have the energy
To turn, as it hangs in the rusty lock.
Just waiting, passively: for fog to disperse.
The time, like words on hold
On the lips of an old woman, flows slowly.
A faint scream, in the torn dawn.

January-2003
Türkçesi: Z. Ali

OUR WALL

To Niyazi and Panikos

Look ! I am just in the middle

ugly, protruded vertebras

of your humpback…

Your rusty, breakable bones

are crackling

under my feet…

You, I

and terrible searchlights

which are illuminating

the desolation's lie…

Look! I am alone on your back…

The people, who created you,

stayed rear and in front of me…

    -They all together looking at their pains

    they have inflicted on each other… -

Eyes blushed from shame

follow my haughty shadow; I feel…

They look trough bullet holes:

frightened and offensive…

Look! I am just in the middle

the one whose steel strong muscles shiever

and, black hairs like thorn

piercing your bloody back's flesh…

I heard your story

from a young man

who went to water his roses

by passport…

Look! We are alone…

Confess it all and tell me…

Tell, who nourishes you?

Tell, how many flags do you serve,

how many people's vampire ?

9- 07-1997 Ledra Palas

DUMANLI TOPRAK

Tülden kanatlarıyla okşayıp Ay'ı
diz/çöktü önünde SİS...
Gece uluyor
kelleşmiş postunu giyinip...
    Hafif bir ürperti, üşüyen tende...
Toprağın dumanı burnunda
ılık bir çorba gibi terliyor, hafiften
    Hafif bir sancı, kabaran kasıklarında...
Tokmağı kopmuş eski kapının
gıcırdayan menteşeleri yorgun.
Paslı kilitte sallanan anahtarın
gücü yok dönmeye...
Sinmiş, bekliyor: dağılsın SİS...
Yaşlı bir kadının dudağını bekleyen
sözcükler kadar ağır akıyor zaman...
    Hafif bir çığlık, yırtılan şafakta...

Ocak 2003

DUVARIMIZ

Niyazi ve Panikos'a

Tam ortasındayım işte
çirkin, omurları fırlamış
kambur sırtının...
Ayaklarımın altında çatırdıyor
paslı, kırılgan kemiklerin.
Sen, ben
ve ıssızlığın yalanını aydınlatan
korkunç ışıldaklar...
Tek başımayım işte sırtında...
Seni yaratan insanlar
arkada kaldılar, ve önümde...
Birbirlerine çektirdikleri acıları
seyrediyorlar birlikte...
Utançtan kızarmış gözler izliyor
mağrur gölgemi; seziyorum
kurşun deliklerinden bakıyorlar
ürkek ve suçlayıcı...
Tam ortasındayım işte,
çelikleşmiş
kasları ürperen
kara kılları diken gibi
etini delen kanlı sırtının...
Pasaportla

güllerini sulamaya giden
adamdan dinledim hikayeni...
İşte yalınızız... İtiraf et
söyle, kim besliyor seni?
Söyle, kaç bayrağın kulusun
kaç insanın vampiri?

                                              09-07-1997 Ledra Palas

Tânia Tomé
Mozambique

Tânia Tomé is a multitalented, award-winner from Mozambique. She is a singer, songwriter, poet, actress, presenter, economist, and socio-humanist. She has worked the world over with social-activism through art. She is the president of the Showesia Association and the Showesia Festival Director. She has released two music CDs *Dreamloving/Sonhamando* and *Lirandzo Blues.*

Tania has also published two books *Agarra-me o sol por trás* and *Conversas com a sombra.* She has released one DVD titled "Showesia."

MUPIPI (MY BIRD)

In your shadow the stars

slowly write themselves

Slowly the stars

Wing wing tendering with wind

Their word shines in the silence

Luminous as the future enters you on wings

And memory has a nest

Arising between twilights

in a harmonic murmur

As you clothe yourself in spring in the depth of autumn

On a morning when the drums

boom out the miracle of the Zambezi

And turning round, you quickly see it,

The entire world you hold inside.

Translation: Erín Moure, Canada

MUPIPI (MY BIRD)

Na tua sombra se escrevem

Lentamente as estrelas

Asa , asa ternurando com o vento

A palavra brilha ao silêncio

Luminosa como o futuro te entra pelas asas

E a memória tem um ninho

Crescendo entre crepúsculos

Num murmúrio harmónico

Como te veste a primavera em pleno outono

Na manha em que os tambores

gritam com o milagre do Zambeze

E olhas esguio a tua volta

O mundo inteiro que tens dentro.

Howard A. Fergus
Montserrat, West Indies

Howard A. Fergus, a Montserratian by birth, is a retired Professor of the University of the West Indies who has acted as Governor of the British colony of Montserrat. He has published widely in the fields of history, education, and literary criticism, including several volumes of poetry.

Obama and Other Poems (2012) is his latest collection.

SOLIDARITY

Montserrat is time zones distant from the Hazara
people, but the wavelengths of oppression encompass
oceans and guerrilla hills. The accent of our tongues
is differently nuanced; yet we who've sung
the mourner's song connect inseparably
by the word made flesh.

I feel the keen of suffering in the ova of my mothers
and the stinging lash of whips on thread-bare backs
under the merciless suns of slavery.

Suffering joins our hands over the bridge
of time and space and bathe them in the gushing
springs of freedom. This word is my hand reaching
out to you and my hammer to smash the fastness
of the strongman, shoot and kill his weapons.

This verse is a voice to swell the shout of freedom,
cause the tyrants' wall to fall, move the hand
of God and good men in Hazara's cause.

Janak Sapkota
Nepal

Janak Sapkota is a haiku poet from Nepal. He won the Smurfit Samhain International Haiku Prize 2006 and the Seventh Annual Ukia Haiku Competition 2009. His recent collections include *Whisper of Pines* [Bilingual edition, Irish versions by Gabriel Rosenstock] (Original Writing, Ireland, 2012) and *A Firefly Lights the Page* [Bilingual edition, Finnish versions by Arto Lappi] (SanaSato, Finland, 2012).

A HAIKU

rusty mailbox
        the last letter-
                almond flower essence

Károly Fellinger
Hungary

Károly Fellinger, a Hungarian poet and local historian from Slovakia was born in Bratislava, on November 20, 1963. He is a winner of the awarded the Golden Opus-prize.

In the 1980s his poems were published in several anthologies. His first collection of verses, *Blackout,* appeared in 1991, which was followed by *The Still Life with the Dead* in 1996. In his volume *The Sky High Wild Pear Trees* (1997) he uses prose and poetry to treasure the myths and tales of the Mátyusföld region.

Since 1993, Károly has edited the quarterly regional journal *Jókai Szó*. His writing on local history, *Sights of Jóka* appeared in 1997 in the *Small Local Historical Library* book series.

His volume of poetry *Nest in the Sky* was published in 2004 and was followed by a book of verses for children: *Grassharp* in 2006 and *Windchasing Round Cloak* in 2008. *The homeless cornflower* appeared in 2009. *Myths and beliefs of Mátyusföld* deals with the fantasy world of Mátyusföld.

Two volumes of children's poetry were published in 2010, the *Wholenut Cradle, Poppy-head Rattle* and *I Have Poppyseed*. The *Luggage Locker* is a selection of poems printed in 2011.

FLOWER SONG

The Hazara dig up their land

although tomorrow they might be

forced to flee from there

but they also know that the land

cannot be blamed,

as it is time to plow,

or to sow,

and tomorrow they will find

reconciliation in the forever fluttering

heart of peace

VIRÁGÉNEK

A Hazarák felássák földjeiket
pedig holnapra talán
menekülniük kell onnét
de azt is tudják, hogy a föld
semmiről se tehet,
hogy itt van a szántás,
a vetés ideje,
s hogy holnapra biztosan
nyugalomra lelnek a béke
örökké verdeső szívében

Alfred Tembo
Zambia

Alfred Tembo is a young African journalist and creative writer. He has published his literary works in Zimbabwe, Zambia, Kenya, Lesotho, and Colombia among other countries before assuming a post at the American Centre-Gweru (Zimbabwe) as the first resident writer.

He has written for the *Daily News* and *Daily News on Sunday* in Zimbabwe and *Ambassador Magazine* (Zimbabwe).

TEARS OF MEMORY

Lost time buried all that could be
Yet tears of seasons-rains
Bears the past caption

Borne from the ancient tales of our time
The Hazara tribe
"In their head they are not defeated"
Papa once told of a story

Tears of time, a memory that soaks them
From peasant to the affluent
We submit to the memories
With every farming season we remember
Our lost kith and kin
Hazara

Hazara! Oh –ye
The undefeated blood
The tribe that lives in everyone's heart
Hazara, a clan of undying poetry and folklores
The tribe who loving people rekindles appreciation
For the written word

Let the next season's tears of memory
Feed nation as we live to imagine untold stories
That were to be told should have lived long

Emilce Strucchi
Argentina

DO NOT

Where does the persecution and death factory exist?
None of us deserve to be expelled from our little place in the world
Do not touch the boys and girls of Hazara
Do not degrade the purity of girls and boys of the whole world

Do not hurt the youth of almond eyes. Didn't you see sadness through the big eyes in the faces of Hazara's people?
You didn't see the sadness of the world
Didn't you see the death's blood sticked in the bodies of Hazara's people? You didn't see death's blood

Do not touch the boys and girls of Hazara
Do not degrade the purity of girls and boys of the entire world

Those who grow up surrounded by almond-trees in flower
Do not deserve either to be expelled from their places or remain lonely, almost dead

Will the poem be useful to human beings pushed to die?
Will the poem be useful to desolation boys and girls?
Will the poem be useful to humillated youth?
Will the poem help Hazaristan's old people?

Do

Not

Touch

Them

NO

Dónde la fábrica de persecución y de muerte?
Ninguno de nosotros merece ser arrancado de su pequeño lugar en el mundo
No toquen a los niños y niñas de Hazara
No denigren la pureza de las niñas y los niños del mundo entero

No lastimen a la juventud de los ojos almendrados. ¿No vieron la tristeza en los grandes ojos de las caras de la gente de Hazara?
No vieron la tristeza del mundo
¿No vieron la sangre de la muerte pegada a los cuerpos de la gente de Hazara? No vieron la sangre de la muerte

No toquen a los niños y niñas de Hazara
No denigren la pureza de las niñas y los niños del mundo entero

Los seres que crecen rodeados de almendros en flor
No merecen ser arrancados de su lugar y tampoco quedarse solos o inermes

¿El poema les servirá para algo a los seres arrancados de la vida?
¿A los niños y a las niñas de la desolación?
¿A la juventud humillada?

¿A los ancianos de Hazaristan les servirá el poema?

No

Los

Toquen

septiembre 2013

Juan Diego Tamayo
Colombia

Juan Diego Tamayo was born in Medellín, Colombia in 1968. He has published a poetry book: *"Los Elementos Perdidos"* (Poemas. 1986- 1998) and is the cofounder of Medellín Festival Internacional de Poesía. He has been invited to several Poetry International Festivals and has given various poetry workshops, and poetic appreciations. His poems have been published in such poetry journals as: *Prometeo, Misterio Eleusino, Imago*, and *Punto Seguido*.

Juan has a Bachelor of Linguistics and Literature (U. P. B) and a M.A. in Hispanic Philology (Instituto de la Lengua Española de Madrid).

I build a house for my dreams

The white flags of love are waving

At dawn's hill I see them

And I see a city that bleeds

Its fear is profound and terrible

You speak to me with words of light

With water syllables

With seed words

I swim in your eyes of freedom

The stars embroider the purity of silence

Construyo una casa para mis sueños

Las banderas blancas del amor ondean

En la colina del alba las veo

Y veo una ciudad que sangra

Su miedo profundo y terrible

Me hablas con vocablos de luz

Con sílabas de agua

Con palabras de semillas

Nado en tus ojos de libertad

Las estrellas bordan la pureza del silencio

Manuel Silva Acevedo
Chile

Manuel Silva Acevedo was born in Santiago, Chile, in 1942.

His books of poems include: *Perturbaciones* (1967), *Lobos y ovejas* (1976), *Monte de Venus* (1979), *Terrores diurnos* (1982), *Palos de ciego* (1986), *Wölfe und Schafe* (1989, Germany), *Desandar lo andado* (1988), *Canto rodado* (1995), and the artists' books *Houdini* (1996) and *Quedar en la tierra* (1997).

Suma alzada, an anthology of his work, was published in 1998, *Cara de hereje* (2000) was adapted into a Commedia dell'Arte performance by La Mancha Theatre Company of Santiago, Chile. His other works include: *Día quinto* (2002), *Campo de amarte* (2008), *Contraluz* (2010) and Lazos *de sangre* (2010).

WOLVES AND SHEEP

There's a wolf inside me
that struggles to be born.
My ovine heart, a stupid creature,
bleeds for it.

Why if I'm a sheep
do I hate my ovine meekness
Why do I curse my peaceful head
back to the sun
Why do I want to choke
on the blood of my grazing stupid
sisters

I was born the wrong way
I was born a sheep
I'm so scared and pathetic
I'm nothing more than a poor sheep
I hate myself
when I hear the wolves
howling in the hills

I, the dreaming sheep,

grazed between the clouds

But one day the she-wolf swallowed me

And I, the stupid lamb,

met the night

the true night

And there in the darkness

inside the she-wolf

I suddenly felt like an evil wolf

If given the choice

I'd be a wolf

But what can I do if this poor skin

does not shine like the black night

if these weak teeth do not bite or shred

If given the choice

I would know how to attack the way I now attack

this wretched, famished, sheepish alfalfa

If given the choice

the silent forests would be my lair

and my ominous howl would make the flocks tremble

But what can be done with this white fleece

How can I transfigure my ovine condition

Manuel Silva Acevedo

I, the obtuse sheep,

fled, trampling my step-sisters

The wolf followed us, panting,

and so I, the prodigal sheep,

stayed at the rear,

The baptist wolf caught up to me

climbed up my back, knocked me down

and sunk his teeth in my neck

Old wolf, he said

Old she-wolf with the skin of a sheep

I want to die with you

I will wait for the dogs

The blood gushed out of me

We looked like a sun with its head

buried in the ground

I was a docile sheep

I always looked at the ground

I was nothing but an ordinary sheep

I was an ovine soul

thirsting for adventure

I was, at heart,

an adventurous sheep

I wanted to become

a lost sheep

I express here my sincere gratitude
to the pious humane eagle
who tore out my jugular with one blow of its beak

It is not necessary to have a master!
Love is necessary, a wolfish love
The most ferocious wolf loves his she-wolf
and scratches and sniffs and jostles
and claws her eyes and listens
and the celestial wolf in the constellations
wags its tail and laughs and waves.

The wolf caught up to the she-wolf
I was watching this
He nudged her from the side with his snout
licked her stomach
and raised his head to howl
I was watching this
I who am no more than a frightened sheep
I can affirm it again
The wolf and the she-wolf were crying

Manuel Silva Acevedo

rubbing against each other's necks
Darkness fell on them
A great silence
There were only stones
and the stars rolled through the sky

Condemned wolf
And blinded wolf
Unlucky wolf
Persevering wolf
Natural wolf
Sheepish wolf
Tooth-snapping shepherd
Howler at stars

To the she-wolf!
shouted the already-drunk men
The beast lifted her ears
and ran to take refuge between my legs
She looked me in the eyes
and there was no ferociousness in her face
To the she-wolf!
Again she heard the shouts nearby

She shook her tail
licked up some water
and I saw her black eyes
outlined against the blue of the sky
Later she fled to the hills
Then I, the unsuspected sheep,
found myself alone before the men
and the black mouths of their shotguns

All the earth is earth for the wolf
If there's rain, mud
If there's sun, dust
And on the road to the hills, the steppes
and in the threshold of the house, the living rock
and the bread's the hardest of breads

I, the silly sheep,
the most ignorant,
I ask myself
Who will take pity on the wolf
and moreover
Who will bury the wolf
when he dies of old age

Manuel Silva Acevedo

myopic and full of lice

It misses you
It looks for you
It investigates you
It pursues you in vain
your hidden name in vain
Don't bear false witness
against the wolf
against the fellow wolf
who howls at his fellow bitch

The flock goes by in a funeral line
and crosses the village and its fountain
The flock goes by, passing in pursuit
of the biggest sheep, the most sheepish
The flock goes by in a somber procession
and behind the tracks the cerberus wolves
leave a trail of saliva
a trace of blood and pollution
The flock goes by and crosses the bridge
The vagabonds and the trains go by

The bitter she-wolf with her teats goes by
The flock goes by, passing slowly
The old she-wolf goes by, the oldest
The black sheep goes by to take shelter
The eternal night goes by, and never lightens
The flock goes and bleats until it is lost

The night fell face down on the flock
The exiled sheep felt the itch
The unfortunate sheep left the corral
It wanted nothing more from this world
but the red breath of the she-wolf

The plague broke out in my family
I saw my clumsy stepmothers
moaning with parched tongues
They died resigned
pressed against each other
I resisted the plague
I fasted, didn't drink water
I didn't accept treatment
And one night the shepherds came
armed with sticks to kill me

Manuel Silva Acevedo

To kill the she-wolf
The only one standing
amid the decimated flock

Leave the she-wolf, to me
Leave the solitary wild beast, to me
Leave the ravaging creature, to me
Leave me the lamb
Leave me the puritan
I am her sacrament
She is waiting for me

My word of honor, said the wolf
I only want to love you, I won't do you any harm
It's okay, there's nothing more to do
stay close to me, replied the lamb
The wolf looked at her with burning eyes
The sheep returned his burning gaze
They stared at each other for a long time
The wolf and the lamb had this dream
One was in the hills where the wind howls
The other in the corral
getting trampled by her sisters

I will no longer belong to anyone

Especially you

Shepherd sleeping against the tree

You shouldn't have trusted this beggar-sheep

You shouldn't have trusted

My stupid watery pupils

You'll be the victim of the bellicose sheep.

There will be no more peace between shepherd and sheep.

The shepherd and the she-wolf searched for the lamb

They climbed the hill in search of the hidden

They found each other, staff and claw

The shepherd was quicker, the wolf defeated

And at the feet of the shepherd, the lost lamb

Came from from the remains of the defeated she-wolf

The shepherd is fooled

The wolf himself is fooled

I will no longer be the sheep in captivity

The sun of the plains

was so warm on my head

I turned into the miraculous beast

I now have my place amid the beasts

Manuel Silva Acevedo

Protect yourself, shepherd, protect yourself from me

Wolf on the prowl, protect me

Translation: Daniel Borzutzky

Elias Letelier
Chile

Chilean-born Elias Letelier worked to establish the External Resistance Fronts in southern Santiago (ADA) in preparation for the Chilean popular uprising.

During that time, he directed over 80 literary workshops with Chilean workers. In November 1981, he left Chile and carried on as Director of *El Siglo* (*The Century News*). From 1981-1983, he worked as a Human Rights Commissioner at Maritime University in Canada, and was a correspondent for several newspapers.

Elias is the publisher and literary editor of Poetas.com, the electronic and paper cooperative publishing house of the Poets of America. He co-founded FEWQ, which later became the Quebec Writers' Federation.

Books: *Mural,* Ottawa: Editorial Poetas Antiimperialistas de América, 2002, *Histoire de la Nuit,* Montreal: L'Hexagone, 1999,

Silence, Montreal: L'Hexagone, 1998, *Silence*, Montreal: The Muses' Company, 1992, *Symphony*, Montreal: The Muses' Company, 1988, *Canciones del Gato*, Santiago: Horizonte, 1976, (this book was seized under the Pinochet dictatorship).

Anthologies: *Freedom, Anthology of Canadian poets for Turkish resistance*. Ottawa: Poetas Antiimperialistas de América, 2006.

Canto a un Prisionero. Antología de Poetas Americanos: Homenaje a los Presos Políticos en Turquía. Ottawa: Editorial Poetas Antiimperialistas de América, 2005.

Anaconda: Antologia di Poeti Americani: Omaggio ai Prigionieri Politici spagnoli detenuti in Francia. Trans. Elisabeta Lasagna; Prefazione di Moreno Pasquinelli. Ottawa: Poetas Antiimperialistas de América, 2003.

Multimedia: *Poemas Escogidos*, Multimedia. Ottawa: Cdpoesia (www.cdpoesia.com), Editorial Poetas Antiimperialistas de América 2002.

Translation: *Farkas, Endre Palabras Sobrevivientes* Trans. Elias Letelier. Ottawa: Editorial Poetas Antiimperialistas de América, 2002.

I SAW

Here another star, flung down,
confused with the dandruff of the jungle,
is turned into a pulp of blood and mud.

Over his extinguished hands
the kiss of the rain falls
and searches for asylum
within the flower that had already died.
No one will sing to him;
he will sleep with his dream
like a rotting leaf in the forest.

Who is my enemy?

Is it my brother, the one
set to dreaming
with a mutilated alphabet?

There is no answer:
like the sawmill worker
melted on the pulley
he left
and he will never come back.

Mohammed Bennis
Morocco

Mohammed Bennis is a Moroccan poet and one of the most important authors of modern Arabic poetry. He was born in Fez, Morocco, in 1948. Mohammed contributes energetically to modern Arabic poetry and since the 1970s has enjoyed a special status in Arab culture.

Muhsin J. al-Musawi writes about him: "Moroccan poet Muhammad Bennis' articulations tend to validate his poetics in the first place, to encapsulate the overlap and contrast of genres in a dialectic that takes into account power politics whose tropes are special. As a discursive threshold between Arab East and the Moroccan West, tradition and modernity, and also a site of contrast and configuration, Muhammad Bennis' self-justifications may reveal another poetic predilection, too."

VIEW

To The Hazara People

Because I move in this venerable orphanbood

I draw from my regions the power

and the power

I said to the carriages

Unite

in the heart

of disaster

I came upon a view of corals there

that took me

to the root of the beginning

where shadows celebrated their silver silence

Whom among you leaves me

these lights' friendship giving my fingers joy

from a single flash of lighting

a cry in the metal chosen for you

For you it ends in death

but that is not death

rather an exodus of colors

from tapping nails

to ocean spry

to figures of dry clay

They said

I don't understand them

Translated from Arabic by Camilo Gomez-Rivas

Károly Sándor Pallai
Hungary

Károly Sándor Pallai is a PhD student at Eötvös Loránd University - Budapest. He consecrates his research to the contemporary francophone literatures of the Caribbean, the Indian Ocean, and the Pacific.

Károly is a member of several international scholarly societies and associations (United States, France, Mauritius, and Australia). He's the conceptor, founder, and editor-in-chief of the international electronic review of literary creation and theory *Vents Alizés*, and founding director of the publishing house Edisyon Losean Endyen.

Károly writes and publishes poetry in French, English, Creole, Hungarian, Spanish, and Portuguese. His collection of poems in French, *Soleils invincibles* was published in 2012; his play, *Mangeurs d'anémones* and his collection of poems in English, *Liberty Limited* were published in 2013.

In acknowledgement of his theoretical, poetical, and editorial work, he was included in the list of "50 Young Hungarian Talents" by the *La femme* magazine. In 2013, his poem « Elle. Seule. » was chosen to participate at the international poetry festival Woman Scream (in collaboration with the French artist Sophie Lartaud Brassart). The Seychellois Minister of Culture awarded him *A Certificate of Ministerial Appreciation* for his activities which promoted the literature and culture of the Seychelles.

DALIL'DERA

Disarmed, abused, executed: we're all peoples of Hazara sharing the doom of enslavement and execution. Our future is quelled, drowned into blood by armor-piercing shells of hatred and exclusion. Crossing nations, ages of gunpowder, limbs ripped off by the drunken haze of history.

Sanguine geographies, tribes, battles and armies, clouds of splinter shouting at skies of oppression. Wizened, cracked exuviae of our liberty judged non accountable by groups of interest, exiled to the railed cots and iron beds of a lunatic asylum smelling urine and vomit. Is this our liberty?

Our tortured, distorted, convulsive bodies have been piled up in the sewers. Are these the funeral honours and the remembrance of posterity that we deserve?

We have a language, let its words roar, squeal and moan the monstrosities of our systematic annihilation. Displaced by force, massacred, we've seen our lands confiscated, our villages deported. Let us be the peace of the world.

These lands are drenched with the silken liquor of our blood, the insane mythologies of extinguishment. Mountains aiming for the heavens, failing histories of uprisings. The barbed wires of a lead-weighted decline transpierce our lungs, giving way to squeaking laments of a century-old mourning.

A people gathered in the internment camps of unending horror. We're the marginalized outlaws, the deprived and despotically exploited, overstrained angels of this contemporary, global orphanage.

We're burning trees of this new, flesh-eating plutonium, the migrating skeletons of genocides and pogroms followed by global silence and a murderous lack of interest.

A history of silence, a culture layed in ruins; our voices have been buried with our decaying, rotten, decomposing bodies but here are here to stay growing louder, calling our tyrants to account at the end of times.

Let our injuries, grieves, howling agonies incise our heartbeats in the collective imaginary, let them etch in the lines of force of our traumatic recollection penetrating the skin of the unconcerned continents.

The book of our body bears testimony to the unforgettable, unspeakable and inconceivable incubus. We're the unrepentant temples outbraving the obduracy of human evilness, the entreating, expiatory protuberances of the holy scriptures.

We're the rended martyrs of despondency, the persecuted Buddhas of savage firing squads, we're the infant Jesus casted to the mauling brutes, the eviscerated Krishnas of benumbing dread. We're the vulnerable saints of oblivion calling out to the world.

We're a tango-coloured renewal, a polliniferous conscience spreading across nations. Our faith and trust are everlasting, our hope is inured. We've earthed up our seeds with the blood carpet of our sacrifice upholstering the valleys. The buds are ready for the efflorescence, bursting into bloom to wash away the sins of this land.

Let our footprints blaze the trail of reconciliation. Let there be light.

Edgardo Nieves-Mieles
Puerto Rico

El poeta y narrador puertorriqueño Edgardo Nieves-Mieles (1957) es autor de 8 poemarios, entre éstos *El amor es una enfermedad del hígado* (1993; 2013), *Este breve espacio de la dicha llamado poema* (2006), *A quemarropa* (2008), *Estos espejos ciegos donde palpita la música del mundo* (2009), *Las ceremonias de la angustia* (2011) y *Con las peores intenciones* (2012). Ha publicado, además, los relatarios *El mono gramático y otros textos* (1995), *El maligno fulgor de la desdicha* (2012), y la novela *Los mejores placeres suelen ser verdes* (2013). Junto a José Liboy-Erba armó a 2 manos otro relatario, *Las aventuras del Pez Gato* (2012). Próximamente otra novela suya recibirá el bautismo de la tinta, *No sé por qué cuando me enamoro tengo pesadillas*. Tanto su obra poética como narrativa ha sido ampliamente premiadas y figura en importantes antologías.

BACHATA PARA UN AHOGADO SIN PAPELES

Sentado en un sillón de mimbre.
Frente a las 78 cartas del tarot.
Alrededor de un tintero.
Encima de mi reloj.
Debajo de mi sombrero.
Sobre el tristísimo pan de cada día.
Derramando rabia y silencio con la paciencia de un santo.
Ahogando cristales de azúcar en la humeante taza del café.
Bebiéndome el universo con los sentidos.
Balbuceando sin sosiego cuánto le amo.
(Por más que lo intento, no consigo desprenderme
de esa terrible imagen que como enloquecida yedra
me clava sus garras en el mismo epicentro de la memoria.
Hablo de sus ojos, de esos 2 escarabajos de duro jade
que con ira implacable no dejan de incendiar
el espumoso adiós de mi definitivo pañuelo.)
¡Qué ardua tarea la mía!

   El sueño huye de mí, se acuesta a mis pies
en sus tranquilas aguas y se duerme.
Ya no me alimento de abrir las páginas del diario

y ver en ellas al mundo y su selva de signos siempre al alcance de la mano.
Ahora miro y veo pasar el plateado fulgor de mis arterias.
Mi esqueleto, esa mariposa de calcio
con una amapola de fuego tatuada en el ala izquierda.
Los regios cordeles de mis nervios donde ahora cuelgan unas prendas íntimas
que no dejan de llorar un agua lenta y obscena en espera, quizá,
de que la violencia de las horas unifique la carne y el espíritu que suele habitarlas.
Una meditabunda camisa que puja y suda complicidad a cántaros.
Las ramitas de mi reverdecido báculo.
¡Mis bolsillos traspasados de deudas y ternura sin remedio!

Ahora que el mar es sólo una gigantesca gota de agua y sal
sembrada de cadáveres que no quisieron comprar boleto de regreso,
la guitarra comienza a deshojar su quejumbroso reclamo.
Como quien al descuido tira semillas sobre el espejo del agua,
así, juntando va los amargos acordes de esa bachata
para uno que se alejó demasiado del conuco
con la ciega certeza de que República Dominicana
y Puerto Rico son de un bote los dos remos.
De que la Virgen de Altagracia protegería los sueños
que mece la yola cuyo costillar es sólo un nido de ruiseñores.
Hablo de ese hermano al que tanto sol gratuito
se le ha enredado en los párpados
estropeándole la brújula del sentido común.

Tras descubrir que el hambre domestica el miedo
pero no acorta las distancias, llora y gime. Gime y llora.
El inclemente arrullo de la incertidumbre le nubla la razón.
Le falta el aire. A sorbitos la vida lo abandona.
(De seguro los golosos bárbaros del ALCA y el ¢apitali$mo globalizado
le han puesto precio a sus órganos tercermundistas.)
Terminará flotando por ahí, como un molusco a la deriva
en ese inacabable cementerio de agua bordado de vértigos y espuma sucia.
Con una extraña flor violeta en los labios
presagiando el cercano matrimonio de la carne y el aire.
Con el vientre hinchado a punto de reventar
para luego dejar al descubierto las riquezas
que la pobreza almacena en el interior de sus vísceras.
Los más voraces cangrejos darán ya cuenta del último
paisaje dormido en los opacos cristalitos de sus pupilas:
esa tan soñada franja verde y firme para los pies que,
adiestrados en la veloz carrera, procurarían burlar el cerco
y las aspas de la libélula de los guardacostas.

   No es culpa mía (pero seguramente lo es) que el tanquero Exxon Valdez
choque con un arrecife y derrame 11 millones de galones de petróleo,
ocasionando con ello uno de los peores desastres ecológicos de la historia
y, de inmediato, el recuerdo de su voz

estremece las ventanas y es como si la primavera
atravesara inmensas pescaderías, desnuda y tiritando de frío.
No es mi culpa (pero sí lo es) que Antonio Gaudí
cruce la calle inmerso en sus cavilaciones
y un imperdonable tranvía lo atropelle.
No es culpa mía (pero seguramente lo es) si cada vez que Pedro Mir
invoque a Walt Whitman (un cosmos, un hijo de Manhattan),
la sangre adquiera cierto rumor de hélices en plena rotación,
de émbolos y poleas, de turbinas incansables y grillos en celo,
y de tanto caminar, a mis viejas huellas le crezcan un par de zapatos
nuevos.
No es culpa mía (pero seguramente lo es) si aún el río murmura
lo que llorando Pablo Neruda le hubiera dicho a Josie Bliss
desde el largo silencio de su ausencia, tras enterrar aquel rencoroso
cuchillo
entre las sordas raíces del cocotero.
No es mi culpa (pero sí lo es) que escribir sobre Atlanta
le duela hasta la yema de los dedos a Juan Antonio Corretjer.
No es culpa mía (pero seguramente lo es) que la soga que ya era fina,
¡ay!, en Medianía Alta partió por lo más finito
y ahora, ¡ohé, ohé!, cuando el travieso vaivén del viento
deja ya de bailar por las más altas palmeras
y en el batey el guabá emite su espantoso silbido
y escapan de los vejigantes los jueyes de más tierna mirada,
es que, con una avispada rabia perfumada de clavos pintada en su
voz,
otra vez Adolfina Villanueva enfrenta la bota

del veremundo terrateniente y los crueles sicarios del poder.
No es mi culpa (pero sí lo es), señor Ministro de Salud,
que, entre tanta lagartija clandestina y viernes colérico,
de repente César Vallejo no tenga siquiera una piedra
en que sentarse y que, injustamente, haya ido a dar,
con sus húmeros mojados a una celda carnívora y voraz.
No es culpa mía (pero seguramente lo es), que, poco antes
de pegarse un tiro en el pecho, Vladimir Maiakovski
haya hecho de su rabiosa espina dorsal una flauta
y que la tocara con ternura nunca antes escuchada
hasta quedar convertido en una nube en pantalones.
No es mi culpa (pero sí lo es) que el comandante Guevara
haya entrado en la muerte para que en el escandaloso concierto
de las cigarras nos siga recordando que no hay que pelear
hasta morir, sino hasta vencer.
Tampoco es culpa mía (pero seguramente lo es) si, de pronto,
el vivísimo y refrescante verde de los árboles
se le vuelve a meter atropelladamente en los ancianos ojos
a Juan Gelman y él se siente feliz que así sea.
No es mi culpa (pero sí lo es) que nos sigamos
haciendo de la vista gorda y optemos por el silencio y el olvido
ante la maravillosa posibilidad de arrebatarles a los verdugos
el cadáver de su nuera María Claudia para que al fin
descanse junto a los suyos, en su tierra.
Tampoco es culpa mía (pero seguramente lo es) que, tras conocer
su verdadera identidad, la nieta robada por la guerra sucia
no pueda mirarle a los ojos y pronunciar

un dulce "¡abuelo, cuánto te he extrañado!"
No es mi culpa (pero sí lo es) que la Srta. Putamuerte,
enamorada de su dignidad para repartir a baldes llenos y de su valor
a prueba de balas full metal jacket, haya venido a buscar a Filiberto Ojeda Ríos.
Sepan todos que al anciano de abuelas barbas no lo mató alguien que desde niño
se acostumbró a contemplar el mundo a través de una mirilla telescópica
en la pantalla de su Nintendo. Alguien que quiso luego disfrutar
lo que se siente al disparar contra un ser vivo: de carne,
huesos, riesgos y convicciones. Alguien que entonces solicitó un empleo
para halar el gatillo caliente cobijado por el infame FBI
y el terrorismo legal del Patriot Act y del Homeland Security.
Alguien que, llegada la tan ansiada oportunidad, no pudo reprimir el escalofrío
de placer casi primitivo electrificándole los microchips de la columna vertebral.
No, al guerrero Filiberto Ojeda Ríos no lo mató
un francotirador del norte escondido en la maleza.
Tampoco lo mató una bala de un rifle M4A1 modificado.
A Filiberto Ojeda Ríos lo mataron la colonia y su maldito perímetro de miedo.
Lo asesinó la guachafita del baile, la botella y la baraja.
Lo mató un bonsái ideológico llamado Estado Libre Asociado.
Lo asesinó tanta alegría con la mirada llena y la cabeza vacía

haciendo fila en Plaza Las Américas para la "Venta del Madrugador".
Lo asesinaron los que hinchan de orgullo sus pulmones
cada vez que nombran "relación digna" a la hipócrita subordinación política.
Lo hicieron ignorando que su plan bonito revolcaría el hormiguero
aquel para siempre fatídico 23 de septiembre.
Que tu hermosa sangre derramada palpita en el filo de un machete.
Que podrán cortar todas las flores, pero no detendrán la primavera.
Tampoco es mi culpa (pero seguramente lo es) que la indiferencia
se despinte las uñas en un extremo de la cama
mientras esa señora espejuelada, de cabellos plateados
y con una cinta métrica alrededor del cuello,
tras echarle la bendición y colmarle de besos,
regaña amorosamente al joven soldado
porque ahora tendrá que coserle la camisa llena de agujeros
por los que su sangre escapa interminablemente.
No es mi culpa (pero sí lo es) que la insolencia
se pinte los labios frente al espejo mientras un niño, todo entusiasmo,
sale corriendo de la tienda con ambos brazos en alto.
En la mano derecha, trae un globo rosado; en la izquierda, uno anaranjado.
Cruza la calle. No ve venir ese Lincoln Mercury
que no logra esquivarle y lo atropella.
Tendido en el suelo, con los ojos vidriosos,
el niño contempla cómo sus preciados globos ganan altura
y se pierden en la distancia azul del cielo sin que pueda ya evitarlo.

Tampoco es culpa mía (pero seguramente lo es) si algún
inescrupuloso mercader de ilusiones (todo sonrisas
estilo agencia gubernamental) te vende visa para ese sueño
de un mundo mejor y tú, hermano, no escuchas que por los labios
de las malignas sirenas escapa una bachata para otro muerto sin
papeles
y te apresuras a seguir tragándote el también traidor anzuelo
sin querer aún darte cuenta que ese mar con 7 tonos de azul
no aguanta un viaje más y que los tiburones
nunca se cansarán de engullir a los tuyos
porque, según cuentan, su carne es la mejor
para conservarle blanquísima la dentadura al espanto.
No es mi culpa (pero seguramente lo es) si en Sudáfrica
el apartheid posibilita que un negro sea blanco de un disparo
y de repente las mansas aves dejan de venir a comer
de mi mano porque esa misma mano recién comienza a chorrear
idénticas gotas de espanto. Espanto, eso digo, interminablemente
espanto.
¡Me avergüenzo hasta las lágrimas!

No es culpa mía (pero seguramente lo es) si estoy hecho de
proteínas
y mermelada, de veredas y almizcles de insospechado origen,
de bosques y banderas ensayando magníficas canciones,
de azúcar y sal repartidos a sobresaltos por igual,
de minutos y alcobas como cucharas recién llovidas,
de excesos y traspiés hasta caer rendido en medio del festín

(¡hay que ver cómo malgasto Chanel perfumando mi falsa
modestia!),
de palabras relucientes como canicas acabaditas de comprar
y que guardo en una lata de galletas al pie del limonero en flor.
No es mi culpa (pero sí lo es) que cada vez que piense en sus pálidas
e inteligentes orejas como si cortase el delicioso y sangriento tallo
de un lirio, me duelan la bragueta y la punta
de este cuerpo enamorado hasta las heces.
 (La veo pintándose las uñas en un extremo de la cama:
yo le ofrecía mi manzana de Adán, y ella,
ella me negaba el perfil de jugoso melocotón que aún esconde
entre sus muslos cuando mis labios se acercan
y, fresco como el invierno de Calgary,
cuelgo mi alma de cada sonido que pronuncio,
de cada sílaba que a sus pies desgrano.)
Tampoco es mi culpa (pero sí lo es) que ese ángel de menta
que vuela en húmedos círculos sin reposo,
termine por descender y colocar en mi mesa
sus alas de madera perfumada por una eternidad
de jazmineros, un higo, 3 claveles y un vaso de leche.
(De inmediato, una nube de acetona
cubre el espeso follaje de mi cabeza caliente.)

   El jardín despereza su prodigio sin compás ni guitarra.
Mi blando corazón de cobre y hojalata resuena.
Le da la bienvenida a la palabra justa y exacta.
Soy y no soy aquél que en vano te ha esperado

junto a las cálidas aguas de la alberca.
Nunca te he visto. Jamás conseguí acercarme lo suficiente.
(Pienso en ello con todas las fuerzas de mi alegría.)
Mis pensamientos se sacuden estremecidos por el misterio,
pero todo es inútil, igual que esa mancha en el césped
que no puede ser otra cosa que un violín sin cuerdas.
(El pequeño Gabriel Alejandro toma impulso
y con sus tiernos brazos rompe el sedoso velo
de la superficie, no sin antes gritar "¡adiós, mundo cruel!")
No tengo tos, pero sólo deseo saludar al muy orondo de mi hígado:
¡Qué tal, imbécil!

    Por el este, el rey anuncia (con entusiasmo casi religioso)
su cúpula de ceniza. Sus trapos de aceite.
Tres pelícanos en majestuoso vuelo,
uno detrás del otro, parten la raya del horizonte.
Como quien, sin aspavientos, prepara otra taza de café con leche,
la más sabrosa (¡ahh, quién osaría tener a menos
semejante bálsamo de Fierabrás!),
prefiero pensar que de seguro se trata de la Sagrada Trinidad,
con todos los emblemas e insignias de sus cargos,
irrumpiendo en este irrepetible jardín de las delicias:
Padre, Hijo y Fantasma Sagrado.
(Al fin el mar se despojará de su amargo y azul antifaz.)
Y yo, con mi nombre y mi suerte de barajas
dejadas caer en medio de la noche,
no me canso de amar a las mujeres

cada vez que me hundo en ella hasta la última gota derramada.
(Después de todo, le amaré como si fuese siempre la primera vez:
columpiando a 4 labios la más traviesa ternura
de este vivísimo anillo que nos ata
el ombligo y la garganta al derecho y al revés.)

El azar transforma a veces nuestros actos
en una soga ceñida ostentosamente al cuello
cual deslumbrante corbata, y de tanto cantar, no tengo ya boca.
Las manzanas se pudren a mi alrededor,
pero hace más de 20 años y todavía no me falla la tonada.

Desde la jaula, los canarios enhebran su canto.
Ya no hay nada más que desnudar.
Respirar puedo ahora en paz y a mis anchas.

Tampoco tengo caspa, pero ¡cómo golpea
esta bestia de lujo que vive, sueña y duerme conmigo!

Fatoumata Ba
Mali

Fatoumata Ba was born in Gabon in November 1974 to a Senegalese mother and Malian father. She's a Sociologist and anthropologist. Fatoumata is well traveled and has seen many different places.

Fatoumata has published poetry *Art Le Sabort,* a Canadian magazine of poetry. She has earned many prizes including: the UNICEF prize of poetry in 1996, and the Francophony Daily (poetry prize) in Mali in 1997.

In 2001, she received the Special Award to the 4th Games of Francophony in Poetry – Ottawa, Canada.

Fatoumata was invited to Medellin in 2007 for the international festival of Poetry and has been published in Prometeo Anthologie (Colombia). She is married and lives in Saudi Arabia with her husband, and their two daughters and their young son.

MEDITATION

If you open your eyes at the evening of your life,
You moreover than to lay down it sun will not have seen anything,
but which spectacle isn't this step?
 Which still unequalled spectacle confusing?

At the beginning all was made up of artifice,
An invitation with torture soft and well elaborated,
Who could have imagined
No suspicion in the speeches

The spider weaves its fabric in most skilful of silences
The hard-working ant leads me with patience
Each day a test
Undergone under the shade of the dictatorship

To go on embers is not an easy thing
In this universe even less
Constant traumatism
Those which remain in are constrained

When little by little the hidden face of the things appears,
When unties itself unrelentingly knots,
That the fog thickens letting show through hypocrisy
Wake up!

What imports time,
Years without confessions
The sun is shining for all
The truth always triumphs

Great regret in this adventure
Not - said will always remain
What is white isn't really
A closed door hides an open one

Only consolation in this episode:
It is not finished, and I believe in God
Who will raise the veil on what really was
Who will raise each workman according to his merits

Let us keep from being malicious
Each Puzzle has its place
Stand to change your destiny

Fatoumata Ba

Vupenyu Otis Zvoushe
Zimbabwe

Vupenyu Otis Zvoushe is a Zimbabwean poet. He spent his happy childhood in Zambia where he attended primary school. A former high school English teacher who writes in his spare time, Zvoushe has yet to publish his poetry in a single volume.

I write to the Hazara people against the persecution they have suffered from time immemorial. I believe in a peaceful world where there is equality and respect of humanity.

MY DEAR HAZARA

Hazara my love, why are you persecuted and killed?
Are you not as beautiful and equal as those around you?
Zipping our sentiments against humanity is our biggest crime
A soul is ruthlessly lost because of downright discrimination
Relentlessly committed by a despotic harrowing mind but,
A light of HOPE and PEACE shall shine for you Hazara my love

Vupenyu Otis Zvoushe

Santosh Alex
India

Santosh Alex is a trilingual poet and multilingual Translator born in 1971 in Kerala. He has an M.A. and PhD. in Hindi Literature. He has two poetry collections Dooram (2008) and *Njan ninakku oru ghazal* (2013) in Malayalam.

Santosh's poems has been translated into Hindi, English, Telugu, Nepali, and Odiya. His poetry has appeared in *Hudson View* (South Africa), *Best Poems Encyclopedia* (New York), *The Single Hound* (USA,) *Rahapen* (Norway), *Sunrise from Blue Thunder- An International Anthology* edited by Ami Kaye, and *Indo Australian*

Anthology of Contemporary Poetry: Vibrant Voices, *The Enchanting Verse*, *Indian Ruminations,* and *Seven Sisters Post.*

He was selected as the poet of the month by the *Single Hound* literary journal (USA) in September 2011.

Dr. Santosh translates post-colonial literature in English, Hindi, and Malayalam. He has been enriching Indian Literature by means of translation for the past 20 years, and has introduced more than 70 writers from five different languages to English, Hindi, and Malayalam.

He has written nine books in Hindi and several English translations, including: *Shuruateim* (poetry of K Satchidanandan), *Dehanthar* (poetry of Savithri Rajeevan), *Samakaleen Malayalam Kahaniyam* (Hindi translation of Malayalam stories), *Aligarh ka kaidi* (a short novel of Punathil Kunhabdullah.) and *Kavita ka girna* (Travel poems of K.Satchidanandan).

Santosh's other translations are *Shelter from the rain* (English translation of Hindi poems of Ekant Srivastava) and *Kavita ke Paksh Mein Nahin.* (Hindi translation of Jayant Mahapatra's poems), *Khamosh muhurth man* (Hindi translations of Malayalam poems of A. Aiyappan).

He has received the Pandit Narayan Dev Puraskaar (2004) and "Dwivageesh Puraskaar" (National Award for Translation) by Bhartiya Anuvad Parishad, New Delhi (2009). His biography was included in the recent edition of *Asian Admirable Achiever* for his contribution to Indian Literature through translation and creative writing. Santosh works as a Technical Officer with CIFT, Visakhapatnam.

AFGHANISTAN

For Kamran Mir Hazar

In the evening
I began to tutor my daughter.
As I was turning the pages of her
english text book
she said, the teacher has instructed
to write an article on Afghanistan .

I remembered that
an article on Afghanistan
was published in a journal sometime back .
I kept it safely in a file
but don't remember where.

Daughter said again
It is being destroyed by bombs.
Schools and colleges are closed.
Isn't it that
the children there too want to study.

I remained silent.

Me, my daughter and Kamran
are waiting for the day

when Surya kiran planes [1]

hover on the Afghan sky.

1: Surya Kiran planes are a part of Indian Defence Force. They are manned by experienced fighter pilots who perfrom breathtaking aerobatic show as part of different celebrations in the country .

Silvana Berki
Albania/ Finland

Silvana (Begotaraj) Berki is an Albanian-Finnish citizen and a social worker in Tampere City, Finland; she is an Albanian-Finnish-English interpreter, the author of two poetic books, the secretary of International Galactic Poetry ATUNIS- world writers' organization, and free-lance reporter in Tampere magazine.
Themes she touches in her poetic writings are an expression of dynamism in national dimension but also universal.

She mostly uses patriotism lyrics, epical and new days poetry of reality and social problems around the world.

Silvana is a mother of two children, ages 24 and 20, one a student at Tampere University and the other in the last year of secondary school.

Silvana is a devoted poet, writing for passion and art, which is why she never compromises with her own opinion when addressing social reality. She sees this as her mission.

I GUESS,

Trust builds a rainbow bridge

We walk to the future, and in the past,

We walk ... In the snow and into dust,

Throught a rainbow bridge,

I guess,

REMEMBER!

I know that the spirit may soon cover darkness,

The world is so cold,

The world has so many shortcomings,

Spider nets many times can also poison you too,

And Yoy stand a morning with empty soul,

Where revenge, hatred, fear begin to cover,

Oh, know that the only antidote is love,

Do not let swim in reverse.

Remember, how good dreams flowrish Aurora`s after rain

Remember when cold water sources, dry throat freshened

War is gaven to us as soon as born,

Remember ... how well do you feel when someone dreamed,

Remember ...

Only then will be able to fight the darkness.

Fight my love the evil, fight.

Remember ... only the kindness.

Silvana Berki

LIKE A BUTTERFLY!

Let me breathe even only for three days,
Only those will suffice
Easily to sit on the eaves,
To Suck flower nectar full of flavor,
Free to fly, without fear in valley,
To set my head in yours lagoon,
To bubble light melody like cataract
To come and to go away in sleep,
There to sow my kisses,
Eggs like a butterfly will release,
In spring will regenerate my dreams,
When frost wild will pass.
Only three days are needed,
Only three days,
Let it remain butterfly in meadow ...
... through the dew,
There to suck your nectar,
Smile with light,
Three days to stay with you, and let alone die.

WHAT MATTER IS JUSTICE!

To me,

All it matter is justice,

I am not saying that you should carry the same values,

All I am saying is;

Justice never wins without a fight.

Didn't Luther King fight for that?

Didn't Mandela protest lifelong prison?

To show the world,

Injustice can't take place!

It is true,

We human been created the law,

And like aristocrat says: we became a law ourselves,

A law, which guide our thoughts when we are in dark,

Which protect our conscious from ego, and a sick pride?

A law which show the right road, when we are lost?

What is law?

A system of thoughts?

All, it matter is justice,

For other things I do not care,

I do not care how many countries you have travelled,

How wealthy you have become,

I don't care for the Saint cross you are carrying …

… when your heart is full of sadistic light.

Today, I am going to surprise
Today, I am not going to thank like the tradition of Christmas demand
Either to cry,
But, I will forgive injustices everywhere in the world,
Only for a night,
…. because is Christmas night
Tomorrow…
I will fight again,
Because to me all it matter is justice,
Fixing the world right!

OUT OF THE SYSTEM

Out of the system,

You felt when a apparel worn in the child`s body,

With ugly words is ridiculed and tortured,

Clotted his mind with snipped "blood,

For…someone is teached,

…and incline to tease!

...

Out of the system,

Feel, when your mind educate cannot as poor,

When little farther, in suburb blinded to see the truth,

No bread,

Homeless,

With outstretched hand in a heavy space, lack of air

Child beggars in impasse,

Dragging are building their life.

Out of the system,

You are,

Do` not think wealth has entered you inside,

You coax a small piece of empty life, because of its what `can meet?

And pleased are saying: I am part of this body institution, give and take ... whatever I want,,,

But in reality,,, nothing tastes!

In reality,,, you feel out of the system where living!

Look,

Somewhere a bit further ... the sound of a rotten cane to the causeway you hear,

Symptoms of paranoia following, hitt from someone,

They steal; kill and you again are rising blinded in your system,

Mort tranquility, pleasure that kills ...

Out of the system,

You are,

Don`t even rank plans with the opposite for the future,

No matter you are inside or outside the country of birth,

Country of origin,

Even, as citizens of a another nation can enter like beggars,

By "extort" taxes collected over the years,

However, after returning home from such an experience,

Once you mature is grilled from political systems,

Threatened with prosecution "International beggars"

You slap the unemployed system, the hopeless...

The system that even though inside, let you outside as beggars!

SINNER!

Ah, you paddle in the ocean,

lonely collides with the waves of the Aegean,

C, whispered Gods in your wet ear this evening,

...and why believ as a pauper in fate of mercy,

Struck the bridge stone of our hearts for not lightning light of our soul,

And we wasted believers dream faded,

Sow a crying song with outstretched hand,

For a few hidden libido loneliness of marriage bed,

Sail, sinful pauper,

sail,

But ... do not fling yourself ecstatic a dream ...

Morning now, wake up!

Hussein Habasch
Kurdistan/ Syria

Hussein Habasch, born in 1970, is a Kurdish poet, from Kurdistan / Syria and now lives in Bonn, Germany.

He writes in Kurdish and Arabic. Some of his poems were translated into other languages such as English, German, Spanish, French, Turkish, Persian, and Uzbek.

Several of his poems were published in more than one international poetic anthology. Hussein published a newspaper in 2001 in

Germany, a monthly cultural newspaper in Kurdish and Arabic under the name of *Avestakurd*.

He wrote these divans:
- *Drowning in Roses*, Azmina Publishing House, Amman, and Alwah Publishing House, Madrid 2002.
- *Fugitives Across Ivros River*, Sanabel Publishing House, Cairo 2004.
- *Higher than Desire and More Delicious than the Gazelle's Flank*, Alwah Publishing House, Madrid 2007.
- *Delusions to Salim Barakat*, Alzaman Publishing House, Damascus 2009.

Festival participation:
-Festival of Kurdish Poetry in the Diaspora/ Bonn 2007
-Festival of Kurdish Poetry in the Diaspora/ Bonn 2009
-Festival of Kurdish Poetry in the Diaspora/ Bottrop 2010
-International Poetry Festival of Medellin/ Columbia 2009
-International Poetry Festival of Granada/ Nicaragua 2010
-Der Deutsch-Arabischen Lyrik-Salon/ Germany 2012
-Der Deutsch-Arabischen Lyrik-Salon/ Germany 2013

Homepage: www.husseinhabasch.com

UMBRELLA

The tree saw two nearly naked children

In the rain shivering from the cold

It ran

It ran fast toward them

Opened its leaves

Stood above them

Like an umbrella.

FORGETFULNESS

When a spike saw the hungry through her eye

It was so sad and said

I wish I were a wheat field

The forest trees heard it and said

We wish our fruits were wheat

The rain also heard it and said

I wish my raindrops become wheat

Dripping through hungry bellies

The dirt heard it too and said

I wish the whole of me became wheat

Even the stones when they heard it said

We wish our hearts become wheat

Only the human heard it and said

I wish.......

But he forgot to finish his sentence!

Hussein Habasch

TWO TREES

The tree under which the two lovers sat underneath

Had a bright smiling face

The tree in whose trunk the snake lived

Had always a pale sad face.

THE LOVE OF TWO TREES

Two trees were madly in love

The vindictive woodchopper

Cut their trunks off

He took them home

By chance the two trees met in the fire place

They embraced happily

And burned together.

Hussein Habasch

A TREE'S DREAM

In a dream a tree saw itself fly
All birds visited the tree in the morning
They gifted it feathers and wings
And made it fly with them.

Translation: Mony Zinati

Lucy Cristina Chau
Panamá

Lucy Cristina Chau was born in Panamá in 1970. She has won the Central American Literature Prize (2010), the National Poetry Ricardo Miró Prize (2008), and the Young Poetry Prize (2006). She earned an English Language Bachelor of Arts from the University of Panama and has been an English-Spanish interpreter since 1995.

Lucy has been a Co-organizer of the Ars Amandi International Poetry Festival in the Republic of Panamá and is a member of the World Poetry Movement.

In 2011, she published a book of short stories, De *la puerta hacia adentro*, and in 2009 the poetry book, *La Casa Rota*.
In 2007, she published two book of poems, La *Virgen de la Cueva* and *IndiGentes* and in 2013 another book of poems, *Mujeres o Diosas* in Costa Rica.

I WISH

I wish I had
at least a religion
some path to walk
with faith
with love
with a god's real commandment.

I wish
but instead
hate disguise
in my prayers,
and I kill
God's name
in every child
Hazara people loses.

I wish
but hate instead
commands
my faith.

A COLLABORATIVE POEM FOR THE HAZARA PEOPLE

Poets Biographies:

- Kamran Mir Hazar, Hazaristan/ page 98
- Jessie Kleemann, Greenland/ page 494
- Siki Dlanga, South Africa/ page 496
- Irena Matijasevic, Croatia/ page 497
- Julio Pavanetti Uruguay/España/ page 34
- Aju Mukhopadhyay, Pondicherry, India/ page 21
- Boel Schenlaer, Sweden/ page 499
- Merlie M. Alunan, Ampatuan, Philippines/ page 501
- Ernesto P. Santiago, Philippines/ page 502
- Rassool Snyman, South Africa/ page 503
- Fiyinfoluwa Onarinde, Nigeria/ page 368
- K. Satchidanandan, India/ page 506
- Ban'ya Natsuishi, Japan/ page 27
- Sukrita Paul Kumar, Kenya/ India/ page 508
- Birgitta Jónsdóttir, Poetician, Reykjavik, Iceland/ page 510
- Zelma White, Montserrat, BWI/ page 512
- Navkirat Sodhi, India/ page 514
- Gemino H. Abad, Philippines/ page 516
- Bina Sarkar Ellias, India/ page 72
- Erkut Tokman, Istanbul,Turkey/ page 342
- Mbizo Chirasha, Zimbabwe/ page 518
- Kamanda Kama Sywor, Congo/ page 383
- Joyce Ashuntantang, Cameroon/USA/ page 519

Jessie Kleemann
Greenland

Jessie Kleemann is a performance artist, poet, and painter born 1959 in Upernavik, Greenland. After a few years theatre training (1977-79) she took up visual art and held several art exhibitions until she switched her main artistic field to performance art.

Jessie has performed internationally as well as in the most remote villages in Greenland. She currently lives in Copenhagen working with painting, poetry, and performance. She is also a regular 'guest-wolf' of the international performance artists-group "The Wolf in the Winter".

Jessie has published poetry in Greenlandic, Danish, and English in her book Taallat, Digte, Poems, and over the years her poetry has been translated into Spanish, Estonian, Norwegian, Icelandic, and Faeroes in anthologies etc.

Siki Dlanga
South Africa

I write a lot. When it's necessary I draw. I have been called a Poet. I have an anthology to show for it. It is called "Word of Worth." I have been called a Writer, an Illustrator, a Banner of Freedom, and a Word Magician. Really all I am is a lover of God, a lover of Africa, a lover of humanity, a lover of justice, and all things beautiful and true. I am bold. I am gentle. I am peaceful. I am a fighter. I am free. It all comes out in my writing. I am South African but in reality, I live in Heaven.

Irena Matijašević
Croatia

Irena Matijašević was born in Zagreb in 1965. She graduated with a degree in English and Comparative literature from the University of Zagreb, Faculty of Philosophy.

Irena was a member of the Presidency of the Croatian semiotic society. She works as an editor on Croatian radio, editing literature and humanistic science. She edits broadcasts on poetry and literature, as well as on human sciences.

Irena's work as a translator is marked by translations of theory, anthropology (Clifford Geertz *Interpretative Anthropology, 2010*) and psychoanalysis (Anthony Elliott *Psychoanalytical Theory, 2012*). Her essays have been published in magazines and newspapers.

Matijašević published three books of poetry: *Seemingly* (2007),

Southern Animals (2010) and *Dennmark H20* (2012).

Her poems have been translated into German, English, Slovakian and Polish.

Irena participated at the second International Festival of Literature, in Ordu, Turkey (2011), the Orient-Occident international poetry festival in Romania (2012), and at several festivals in Croatia.

Boel Schenlaer
Sweden

Boel Schenlær b.1963 Poet – translated into 10 languages
Member of The Swedish Writer´s Union.

Editor and translator of the poetry magazine *Post Scriptum*, which presents poems from several countries, mostly in translation.

Founder of the Södermalms Poesifestival, 11th anniversary, 2013.
Founder of the poetrystage PoesiOnstage, 2002.

Awarded the Prins Wilhelm stipend 2010 and
2011 stipend from Fredriks Ströms Minnesfond.

Current work:

Nomad in Exile, translation to Farsi by Sohrab Rahimi, to be published in summer 2013.
I Dream of Blood, Symposion Förlag, Sweden, to be published winter 2014.

Franz Kafka, A Portrait, H. Strom Förlag, to be published in winter 2014 in the series "Litterära profiler".
Nomad in Exile, translation to English by Alan Crozier. to be published in the U.S. in 2015.
Fresk, collection of poetry, New edition, spring 2010, DejaVu Förlag
Det Skarala, anthology, spring 2010, H:stöm Förlag
Nomad in Exile, poems in transalation, to Chinese. *Poetrymagazine* in Beijing, China, spring 2010. 14 poems translated by Mindy Zhang.

Festival Appearances:
Zagreb, Swedish Week, April 2013, Poetry Exchange/Södermalsm Poesifestival
Druskninikai, Lithuania, September 2012
Curtea de Arges, Romania – Poetry Nights, July 2013
St:Anza, Scotland Poetryfestival 2012
Zagreb, Croatia - Writer's Union och Universitetet i Zagreb, october 2011 - chapbook Nomade in Exile published in Croatian
Struga, Macedonia, August 2011
Casa de Poesia, Costa Rica, May 2011 - Nomade in Exile published in Spanish in translation by Elda Garcia Posada.
Struga, Makedonien, August 2010
Zagreb, Croatia, June 2010 - Poetry exchange Stockholm/Zagreb
Bratislava, Slovakien, October 2009

Karlek Som Fobi - collection of poetry/ *Love as Phobia*, PS. Förlag 2007
Nomade in Exile - collection of poetry - 2012, Symposion Förlag.

Poetry translated into English, Arabic, Lithuanian, Russian, Chinese, Macedonian, Slovak and Croatian.

Merlie M. Alunan
Philippines

Merlie M. Alunan lives in the Tacloban City, Leyte, Philippines. She taught Literature and Creative Writing at the University of the Philippines Tacloban College. Now retired, her work as a poet has been recognized by the Palanca Memorial Awards for Literature seven times.

She was a Fellow of the Ananda Coomaraswamy Foundation of the Sahitya Akademi in 2011 and traveled to ten cities to read her poetry as part of her duties. On July 26, 2013, she received the Sunthorn Phu Literary Award from the Thailand Ministry of Culture, representing her country among other ASEAN poets.

Ernesto P. Santiago
Philippines

Ernesto Pangilinan Santiago is a Filipino immigrant, poet, and the author of a poetry book *The Walking Man*, published in 2007, by Outskirts Press. He's also the editor of *The Sound Of Poetry Review*.

His awards include an "Award of Excellence" in the March 2008 Poetrysoup International Poetry Contest, USA, an Honorable Mention winner in the 11th Mattia International Poetry Competition 2008, Canada, a Grand Prix Orient-Occident Des Arts 2008 Internationale Laureate, awarded at the 12th International Poetry Festival Orient-Occident Curtea Des Arges: Poetry Nights 1001 Poems, by L'Acadamie Internationale Orient-Occident, Fondation et Organisation Culturelle d'Utilité Publique, Romania. He received the Nosside Menzionati award in the XXIV Premio Internazionale di Poesia Nosside 2008, Reggio Calabra, Italy. He's a member of Shadow Forest Authors. Ernesto lives and works in Athens, Greece.

Rassool Snyman
South Africa

Mary Smith
Scotland

Mary Smith is a writer, freelance journalist and poet based in Dumfries & Galloway, southwest Scotland.

She worked in Pakistan and Afghanistan for ten years, where she established a low-key mother and childcare program providing skills and knowledge to women health volunteers in Hazaristan and in

Mazar-i-Sharif. She feels very privileged to have had the opportunity to live and work in Afghanistan and spend so much time with ordinary women living extraordinary lives.

Her experiences of living there inform much of her writing. She has written a narrative non-fiction account of part of her time in Afghanistan in *Drunk Chickens and Burnt Macaroni: Real Stories of Afghan Women*. It offers an authentic insight into how ordinary Afghan women and their families live their lives beyond the headlines and political posturing. Her novel, *No More Mulberries* is also set in Afghanistan.

Mary Smith's poems have been widely published in magazines and anthologies and her first full poetry collection, *Thousands Pass Here Every Day* was published in 2012 by Indigo Dreams. The wide-ranging collection includes memories of childhood and family to those inspired by her time in Afghanistan.

Now back in Scotland, Mary continues to keep in touch with Hazara friends both in Afghanistan and around the world.

Mary's website is at www.marysmith.co.uk

K. Satchidanandan
India

K. Satchidanandan, perhaps the most widely translated of contemporary Indian poets, has twenty-three collections of his poetry in eighteen languages including English, Irish, Arabic, French, German and Italian. His book *While I Write: New and Selected Poems* (Harper-Collins) came out in 2011.

Satchidanandan writes poetry in Malayalam, and he writes prose in Malayalam and English. He has more than twenty collections of poetry, besides several books on travel, plays and criticism as well as translations of poetry from around the world, including five books in

English on Indian literature. He has represented India in many Literary Festivals and Book Fairs across the world including in Lahore, Abu Dhabi, Sharjah, Dubai, Damascus, Berlin, London, Manchester, Liverpool, Wales, New York, Washington, Hay, Paris, Frankfurt, Bonn, Leipzig, Beijing, Shanghai, Rotterdam, Medellin, Sarajevo, and Moscow.

Satchidanandan is a Fellow of the Kerala Sahitya Akademi and has won twenty-seven literary awards including the Kerala Sahitya Akademi awards four times, the Gangadhar Meher National Award (Orissa), the Kusumagraj National Award (Maharashtra) and the NTR National Award (Andhrapradesh) besides a Knighthood of the Order of Merit from the Government of Italy and the India-Poland Friendship Medal from the Government of Poland. A film on him, *Summer Rain* was released in 2007.

Sukrita Paul Kumar
India

Sukrita Paul Kumar, was born in Kenya and lives currently in Delhi, writing poetry and teaching literature. An Honorary Fellow of the prestigious International Writing Programed, University of Iowa (USA), Cambridge Seminars and a former Fellow of the Indian Institute of Advanced Study, Shimla, she was also an invited poet in residence at Hong Kong Baptist University.

A recipient of many international fellowships and residencies, she is Honorary faculty at the Durrell Centre at Corfu (Greece). Her books of poems in English include *Without Margins* and *Folds of Silence* in addition to two bilingual collections *Poems Come Home* (with translations by Gulzar) and *Rowing Together* (with Savita Singh). She was the Guest Editor of *Crossing Over* (University of Hawaii). A number of Sukrita's poems have emerged from her experience of working with homeless people, Tsunami victims, and street children.

Amongst others, Sukrita's major critical works include *Narrating Partition*. Her edited/co-edited books include *Speaking for Herself: Asian Women's Writings* (Penguin) and *Cultural Diversity in India* (Macmillan India). She is also a translator and an artist.

Birgitta Jónsdóttir
Iceland

Birgitta Jónsdóttir is an Icelandic poet and is currently serving as a member of the Icelandic Parliament for the Pirate Party and is one of its founders. Birgitta is also the founder and Chairperson of the International Modern Media Institute, better known as IMMI. She specializes in lawmaking for the 21st century.

She has worked as a volunteer and activist for various organizations including WikiLeaks, Saving Iceland, and Friends of Tibet in Iceland.

She carries on being an activist in Parliament, a Poet, and a Pirate. She organized Iceland's first online broadcast in 1996, was the first female Icelandic web developer, has worked as a poet since she was 14 when her first poem was published, and has worked as a publisher in cyberspace since 1995.

Zelma White
Montserrat, BWI

Zelma has over twenty-seven years of experience in Education; seventeen years as a teacher and eleven years as an educational leader. As an Education Officer she has supervisory responsibility for the primary schools on the island.

She once served as secretary of the Montserrat Union of Teachers and has been a preacher and leader within the Methodist Christian Community for over twenty-five years.

Zelma earned her Diploma in Teacher Education from Antigua State College; her Bachelor's Degree from The University of Technology in Jamaica and her Master's Degree from the University of Warwick in the UK. She also has an Associate Degree in Ministry and a Diploma acquired by preachers completing a course of study.

Forced by the volcanic eruptions that started in 1995 to evacuate from the eastern part of Montserrat (Harris) where she grew up, she now lives in the northern part (Judy Piece) with her husband Reuel and son Ramiah.

She sees effective education as very important and finds relaxation in movies, music, dance, drama, novels, poems, and short stories that promote becoming a better person and making ethical decisions. Her aspirations include publishing books of poems and short stories.

Navkirat Sodhi
India

Navkirat Sodhi has published two collections of poetry. They are titled *Un* and *If and I*. She has read at poetry festivals in Kerala and Hyderabad and her work has appeared in literary journals like *Prairie Schooner, The Delinquent, Equinox, Indian Literature, Private, Muse India* and *Canon's Mouth*.

She is presently working on her third book, alongside a transcreation of the *Adi Granth*. Navkirat studied journalism at the University of Westminster, London, and English Literature at the Delhi University. She has worked as a journalist and researcher prior to this and written on art, travel, fashion, health, and food. She lives in New Delhi.

Gémino H. Abad
Philippines

Gémino H. Abad, University Professor emeritus of literature and creative writing at the University of the Philippines, is a poet, fiction writer, and literary critic and historian, with various honors and awards. In 2009 he received Italy's Premio Feronia for his *In Ordinary Time: Poems, Parables, Poetics* (2004), translated into

Italian by Gëzim Hajdari and Amoà Fatuiva under the title, *Dove le parole non si spezzano* (Where No Words Break).

He has to date thirty-six books to his name. *Care of Light* (2010) is his eighth poetry collection, and *Imagination's Way: Essays Critical and Personal* (2010), his eighth collection of critical essays; he also has two collections of short stories, *Orion's Belt* (1996) and *A Makeshift Sun* (2001).

He is also known for his three-volume historical anthology of Filipino poetry in English: *Man of Earth* (co-ed., Edna Zapanta Manlapaz; 1989), *A Native Clearing* (sole editor, 1993), and *A Habit of Shores* (sole editor, 1999).

With *Hoard of Thunder* (2012), comprising stories over 1990 to 2008, he completes the six-volume historical anthology of Philippine short stories in English: the first two-volume set, *Upon Our Own Ground* (2008), comprises stories over 1956 to 1972, and the next set, *Underground Spirit* (2010), stories over 1973 to 1989.

Dr. Abad obtained his Ph.D. in English at the University of Chicago in 1970, and continues to teach at UP where he has served as Secretary of the University, Vice-President for Academic Affairs, and Director of the U.P. Creative Writing Center (now an Institute).

Mbizo Chirasha
Zimbabwe

Mbizo Chirasha is an internationally acclaimed performance poet, writer, and creative projects consultant. He is widely published in more than seventy-five journals, magazines, and anthologies around the world. He was the poet-in-residence from 2001-2004 for the Iranian Embassy and the UN Dialogue Among Civilizations Project.

Mbizo was the official performance poet of the Zimbabwe International Travel Expo in 2007, the Poet in Residence of the International conference of African culture and development, (ICACD), 2009; and official Poet of the Sadc Poetry Festival, NAMIBIA 2009.

A delegate to the UNESCO photo novel writing project in Tanzania, Mbizo is the Official poet in residence for the ISOLA/ international conference of oral literature 2010 in Kenya. Mbizo is widely profiled in both local and international media sources. His poetry books include *Good Morning President*, *Whispering Woes of Ganges,* and *Zambezi*. Mbizo Chirasha the Founder and Creative Director of the "Girlchild Creativity Project" and the newly founded Urban Colleges Writers Prize.

Joyce Ashuntantang
Cameroon/USA

Dr. Joyce Ashuntantang was born in Kumba Town, Cameroon. She is presently an Associate Professor of English at the University of Hartford, Connecticut.

An actress and poet, she is the author of Landscaping *Postcoloniality: the Dissemination of Anglophone Cameroon Literature* (2009) and *A Basket of Flaming Ashes* (2010). Her poetry has appeared in anthologies such as *Reflections: An Anthology of New Work by African Women Poets*, *World Poetry Almanac 2011,* and *We Have Crossed Many Rivers*: *New Poetry from Africa*. She earned a B.A. in Modern English Studies from the University of Yaoundé, a Masters in Librarianship from the University of Wales, U.K., and a PhD in English from the City University of New York. She blogs her world at www.joyceash.com.

A COLLABORATIVE POEM FOR THE HAZARA

Sitting in front of a computer
exploring a world that is not necessarily out of my access
Or close to my own moment of poetry,

- Does poetry have anything to do with my people, the Hazara?
An email sent by a poet, a permanent resident of exile

Ameer of Afghanistan has sold ten thousand Hazara captives as slaves.

- can't this news from October 1893 be part of a poem?
Kamran Mir Hazar, Hazaristan

Your name as a Name could not have been pronounced or said
before the year 1721 in Kalaallit Nunaat, Greenland
at which point was not even known as the Land of the people, the Inuit
Ameer your name sounds like Amee'q which means, Your skin has been taken off of you
Ameer, your skin, where is it and who took it?

Hazara women and men like children

or like my Aanaa   Grandmother or even my Aataa Grandfather

Asassara Asasara Hazara Haza'zara

means I love You Asasara Hazara.

Jessie Kleemann, Greenland

Darkness cannot hide

Your comely face

Evil cannot kill your name

He hears it in a thousand

Cries

Your enemy does not sleep

His bed is the grave

His sheets are death

He cannot shut his eyes

He sees the faces

Of the beautiful

Wondering

Beyond

The borders of their homes

Looking for hope

Looking for home

Hazara

Your name will not be erased

It has been made known to the ends of the earth

Hazara

Your name cannot be erased

Now it is in the prayers of every language

Hazara

Heaven knows your name

Every hair that has fallen off your head

Will be answered for

Hazara

The hatred of your enemies

Has won you the love of the world

Hazara

Hear me when I say

You shall live

You shall live

Siki Dlanga, South Africa

I only know that

suffering must stop

it should stop once

in time

and in certain places.

in the meanwhile

we suffer

knowing it has to stop.

o what a difference between these

two words

between has to and actually
what we have now

is only a hope
such a big word
i ask
and you reply
please

Irena Matijasevic, Croatia

The Hazara people's voice
is the cry of the poet
exclaiming verse by verse
that opens their eyes and ears
to the suffering of people
who they are seeking to erase
until they remove their skin.

The Hazara people's voice
is the force of the poet
joining his pen to other pens
to plant their looks
of green branches
with their fruits of hope
that would stop the pain.

The Hazara people's voice
stands besides the poet
to reclaim the world
to curb the massacres
no more blood running
and that people are not pushed
to the pits of oblivion.

The Hazara people's voice
belongs to all of us
poets who fight
with pen and word
for human rights
for peace and justice
for a free world.

The Hazara people's voice
is mine and yours.

Let us unite all voices
in a single, powerful scream
that shake the foundations
of all the powerful men
until they bite the dust.

Julio Pavanetti Uruguay/España

It is the voice of the poets voice of Peace voice of love

for the Hazara people appealing to all who have been
so far persecuting them, appealing to all humans throughout
the globe to put a stop to it mainly because we are humans;
not dogs who chase and kill other dogs who enter their territory.
With wonderment we observe that the persecutors are from their
own territory, the sufferers suffer in their own territory;
after aeons of development of civilisations how can men be inferior to dogs?

Aju Mukhopadhyay, Pondicherry, India

I dedicate the future

and all the collected

bowls of water

and the imaginary raindeer

and the children´s red noses

and the benefits of social security

the forests of tomorrow

the gold and the silver

in human tears

and all of the rememberance

of healing and sorrow

to the Hazara people.

Boel Schenlaer, Sweden

Who ordered the killing? Whose hands acted the deed—

let us make that name known with our words.
 Let shame and dishonor fall upon that name,
and then follow him to his grave.
To him and his kind who continue to live
and breathe on this world, let rice turn to sand
in their mouth, water into bile. Let the tears
of widows and orphans, lovers and friends,
drench their sleeping mats every night.
May their dreams swarm with the cries
of the murdered. Cram their sleep
 with nightmares. No mercy.
Wherever they go, blood will trail
them forever with its stench.

Merlie M. Alunan, Ampatuan, Philippines

- what I like to smell, while traveling from Bamiyan to Kabul is apple,
not the Taliban infection that abides for three centuries

Kamran Mir Hazar, Hazaristan

... but I am free Hazara,
full of opportunities.
I exist, 'cause I exist
to inspire embracing of
life through our differences.
Ah, the courage to serve peace,
let it be my price, freedom!

Ernesto P. Santiago, Philippines

On distant shores we all sit

A slow awakening humanity

Before time and tide

Fate and destiny we sit

Apart yet together

Bound by common purpose

And similar dreams

Watching the bloodmoon

From its perch in the heavens

Drip crimson radiance onto the people of Hazara

Drip

Drip

Drip

Will justice move from its frozen throne

Raise its hand

And intervene

Make life better

End the pain and misery

Of a people suffering in a cruel world

Where none care

As they go about their lives in ignorance

With dead hearts and blind eyes

Doomed to letting evil flourish

Because they do nothing

But wait… wait… wait, there is hope yet

Those who wield their words

Their poems

Their stories

As sharpened swords

Will slice through the ropes of oppression

That bind tightly the people of Hazara

Change will come

Riding on storms

Of words and poems

Heed ye the ways of the past

History marches relentlessly

Reducing oppressors to but dust

Even a bloodmoon must set

And the sun rise in the morrow

Thus is change inevitable

And freedom made manifest

*** Rassool Snyman, South Africa ***

I know a man

I know a face

I don't know about colours,

All I know is the man with a face

black, white or red

I know the man in whose vein blood flows.

Nature and arms align against the man I KNOW

Cruelty and knocks on my brothers door

Becoming a wasteful sojourner at his door
Tearing apart centuries moulded by the fingers of love.

I weep and mourn with the man that I KNOW
Whose presence I carry everywhere I go
I am a man, my colour does not make me one
I am a man because I am.

I am Hazarian
Across the ocean
I speak for our homeland
Our earth beguiled by our wickedness.

MAN will not fade out
HAZARA LIVES ON...
In the agonies of death
with the collaboration of nature

OUR homeland stands steadfast
In the face of evil
In the wrath of nagging gun
In the inferno of wickedness.

Shut up!
LET ME BE!
Harm the ARMS with your will and Words

Brother please HARM the Arms that HARMS HAZARA my native land.

Fiyinfoluwa Onarinde, Nigeria

Why?
If your soul - and mine -
shivers, splinters as they kill
with cowardly bombs
our brothers, sisters, fathers,
leave mothers awash with grief;
if our souls weep and rage
against these horrors, why
do our leaders around the world
simply shrug
and turn away?

Mary Smith, Scotland

I am the hunted Hazara,
I am the fallen Buddha of Bamiyan,
the innocent's blood on the nascent snow,
the stilled laughter of the blue Lazir,
the wounded wing of the refugee bird,
the chilling tears of the many-hued mountains,
a veil on fire, a wounded horse's endless neigh
from the Shah Tigh pass,
two eyes floating on the waters of Band-e-Amir
the almond that has ceased to blossom.

I have been on the run for decades now,

evicted from my home, cut off from my kin,

even my dreams have whip marks,

and my memories are maimed.

Give me my life , my freedom,

my beautiful land of hills and vales,

my rivers, my sculpted kindness,

my caved love, my Buddha you slew.

K. Satchidanandan, India

彼らは火だった

彼らは水だった

知恵と愛の十字路で

いま彼らは廃墟

彼らは破片

忘却の穴倉のなかで

They were fire

they were water

on the crossroad of wisdom and love

now they are ruins

now they are fragments

in the cave of oblivion

夏石番矢□日本

Ban'ya Natsuishi, Japan

Marking an end
to the long night of oblivion,
the dream of freedom is now visible
perhaps a silhouette of promise
A dream yet to be dreamt

The arrow of light
Rises from the white hole
At the end of the tunnel
Splitting the darkness into
10,000 screams of Hazara captives
Sold as slaves in 1893

Birthing and dying sounds
incubating and gestating
babies born in anguish
and the emerging poems
paving the way to
dream the dreams
of homing …

Sukrita Paul Kumar, Kenya/ India

History is carved from
our collective memory.
We are free
to shape the
future.

The word is creation
-powerful magic.

I carve into the invisible walls
of the internet
a new path
a new way
for the future to unfold
for the people of Hazara.

We have seen you now
you are no longer lost in history
you are now living in our collective memory.

Tells us how the blueprint of your future
unfolds in dreams.

Birgitta Jónsdóttir, Poetician, Reykjavik, Iceland

Sorry,
I was not aware
until the poetic call.
Now I care
on my empathetic knees I fall
to share
Hazara,
Forever etched on my mind

Zelma White, Montserrat, BWI

With lashes

Eyes only shut

So they can dream

> *Navkirat Sodhi, India*

Is it we only dream

Of peace and goodwill among men?

O Hazara, O Filipinas!

Our humanity is our heartland,

Singular and whole

  And invincible!

O Lord God, Word alive,

Let fall from us all our words,

Cumulus of pride, ash of despair;

Be silence of earth, sky, sea,

Our vestment and prayer now.

      Where are the syllables

To sound the gorges of our greed?

Where the flaming writ to scour

Stark deserts of our desire?

Where the letters to forge our creed?

      O teach us again,

Lord God, Word alive,

Both scripture and deed

Of our infrangible Communion __

Wine of twilight in our mouth,

Blood of sunset through our heart.

Gemino H. Abad, Philippines

a hymn for Hazaras
a hymn for humanity

when racism is indictable
when unity is sine qua non
when hearts open wide for all
when wisdom dawns

only then shall we be civilized
only then shall hope be realized

you and I are ever one
let us claim our birthright
let us all be Hazara,
let us all unite.

Bina Sarkar Ellias, India

My hymn is
The catharsis of humanity:
Revealing the scream of the Hazaras
Those genuine voices of poetry: Our wisdom of
Love, loveable loveliness
Can help to stop the blood of innocent people?
Open your heart to the freedom of Hazara

Love is innocent
To love someone is humane
So where are you to be sane?
Not to kill but unite
Our peaceful demand for future!

Erkut Tokman, Istanbul, Turkey

My ink is a flood eroding sediments of tyranny
my pen is bullet splitting propaganda rocks
iam poet whose fontanelle was bleached in pots of metaphor
my verses are lotion drying political gangrene

Mbizo Chirasha, Zimbabwe

Freedom is a source of growth and development for mankind
May the passion for justice and the love of the truth guide us
Towards the achievement of collective happiness.

Kamanda Kama Sywor, Congo

Near Siah Chob Village
Your face sings a defiant song
Hazara! Hazara! Hazara!
And the refrain echoes in bodies
From Khawat through Chardeh
From Mirasi Valley to Banyam.
Your mismatched shoes are
The arrows for the tiny bows
No one can steal your sun

No winter can cheat your dreams

We may never know your name

But the language of your face

Is our grenade on their parade!

Joyce Ashuntantang, Cameroon/USA

An open letter from 354 noted Poets including Nobel, Pulitzer, continental and national literary prize winners as well as presidents of international poetry festivals, presidents of PEN clubs, and writers associations from 96 countries

AN OPEN LETTER FROM WORLD-WIDE POETS ADDRESSED TO WORLD POLITICAL LEADERS

Dear Sirs and Madams,

After more than a century of systematic crimes such as genocide, slavery, sexual abuse, war crimes, and discrimination, being a Hazara still appears to be a crime in Afghanistan and Pakistan. As recently as Saturday February 16, 2013, more than 300 Hazara men, women, and children were killed or injured in a massive bomb blast in the Center of Quetta, Pakistan. This followed a similar attack a month earlier, on January 10, 2013, when more than one-hundred Hazaras were killed in another bomb blast in the same city.

In the past few years, more than a thousand Hazaras were killed in similar attacks in Pakistan alone.

Today, even in their homeland, Afghanistan, Hazaras are not safe. Every year, they are attacked by Afghan Kuchis who are backed by the Taliban and the Afghan government. Hazara roads are blocked by Taliban gunmen. Hazara cars are halted and its passengers are killed.

In the center of Afghanistan, where a huge population of Hazaras are marginalized, they do not have access to basic legal rights. They still suffer systematic discrimination and Taliban attacks. As a result, millions of Hazaras have fled to numerous countries as refugees or asylum seekers, frequently living in terrible conditions.

The Hazara indigenous people made up nearly 67 percent of the population of Afghanistan prior to the 19th century. In that century, they were subjected to genocide and enslavement twice. They were forced to flee most of their land, located in the south of modern Afghanistan. More than 60 percent of them were killed and thousands were sold as slaves.

Afghanistan's entire 20th century history has been marked by killings of Hazaras and systematic discrimination against them. On February 10 and 11, 1993 in the Afshar area of Kabul, the Mujahadeen government, and its allies exterminated and left injured thousands of Hazara men, women and children. In August 1998, the Taliban killed more than ten thousand Hazaras in the northern city of Mazar-i-Sharif. Similar bloodbaths quickly spread to other parts of Afghanistan. Destroying Hazara history and promoting an inaccurate, demeaning history of their culture have been further strategies, in addition to violent crimes. For example, in March 2001, the Taliban notoriously destroyed the ancient Buddha sculptures of Bamiyan which were principal symbols of Hazara history and culture, and one of the most popular masterpieces of the oral and intangible heritage of humanity. Such is the history of two centuries of crimes against the Hazara, and from which they still suffer.

Therefore, we poets from around the world declare our solidarity with the Hazara people and ask you world leaders to take the following steps to properly insure the security and safety of the Hazara people and culture:

1: Declare a state of emergency regarding the Hazara state of affairs, as authorized by the Convention on the Prevention and Punishment of the Crime of Genocide.

2: Apply diplomatic pressure on both the Afghan and Pakistani governments to immediately cease acts of discrimination against the Hazara and to stop supporting terrorist groups who commit violent acts against them.

3: Ask the Refugee Convention's state parties to protect Hazara asylum seekers and grant them asylum.

4: Establish an international truth Commission to investigate crimes against the Hazara.

5: Open comprehensive cases concerning genocide and gross human rights violations in international courts such as the ICC.

6: Over 150,000 international troops are in Afghanistan. They must ensure the safety of the Hazaras before they leave Afghanistan.

7: Appeal to international media to investigate and report on activities against the Hazara, particularly in Afghanistan and Pakistan.

Poets Around the World
Signatures with names, positions, and countries:

1. Fernando Rendón, Poet, editor, and director of International Poetry Festival of Medellin (Colombia)
2. Kamran Mir Hazar, Poet, journalist and webmaster (Hazaristan)
3. Lello Voce, Poet (Italy)
4. Gabriel Rosenstock, Poet (Éire/ Ireland)
5. Irena Matijašević, Poet (Zagreb/ Croatia)
6. Pitika Ntuli, Poet, writer and sculptor (South Africa)
7. Dean Hapeta aka Te Kupu, poet, and musician (Aotearoa, NZ)
8. Dairena Ní Chinnéide, Poet (Ireland)
9. Jack Hirschman, Poet (San Francisco in the United States)
10. Agneta Falk, Poet (San Francisco in the United States)
11. Janak Sapkota, Poet (Nepal)
12. Boel Schenlaer, Poet (Sweden)
13. Ershad Mazumder, Poet (Bangladesh)
14. Alexander Gorsky, Poet, writer, journalist (Ukraine)
15. William Masore, Poet (Kenya)
16. K. Satchidanandan, Poet (India)
17. Thór Stefánsson, Poet (Iceland)
18. Hemant Divate, Poet, Editor, Publisher and Translator

(Mumbai, India)

19. Attila F. Balázs, Poet, editor, Publisher and Translator (Slovakia)

20. AB-ART Publishing house (Bratislava, Slovakia)

21. Enikoe Thiele, Poet, translator (Austria)

22. Alireza Behnam, Poet and journalist (Iran)

23. Mohammad Sharif Saiidi, Poet and journalist (Afghanistan/Sweden)

24. Jüri Talvet, Poet (Estonia)

25. Maggie Cleveland, Poet (Massachusetts, US)

26. Julio Pavanetti, Poet, President of Liceo Poético de Benidorm (Uruguay/Spain)

27. Angelina Llongueras, Poet, Barcelona (nowadays a member of the Revolutionary Poets Brigade in San Francisco, US)

28. Amir Or, Poet and editor (Israel)

29. Fahredin Shehu, Poet and Writer (Prishtina, Kosovo)

30. Andrea Garbin, Poet (Mantova, Italy)

31. Jean-Claude Awono, Teacher, editor and President of La Ronde des Poètes, Cameroon and Festival international de Poésie des Sept Collines de Yaoundé, Festi7 (Cameroun)

32. George Grigore, Poet (Bucharest, Romania)

33. Neeli Cherkovski, Poet (USA)

34. J. K. Ihalainen, Poet and publisher (Finland)

35. Hooman Azizi, Poet (Iran)

36. Maryam Hooleh, Poet (Iran)

37. Philip Hammial, Poet and sculptor (Australia)

38. Rati Saxena- Poet, kritya international poetry festival (India)

39. Bina Sarkar Ellias, Poet, editor, designer and publisher (Bombay/India)
40. Mahmoud Abuhashhash, Poet (Palestine)
41. Julia Kissina, Writer (Germany/Russia)
42. Zelma White, Poet (Montserrat, B.W.I)
43. Merlie Alunan, Poet, Essayist, Teacher of Literature (Philippines)
44. Stanka Hrastelj, Poet and writer (Slovenia)
45. Zingonia Zingone Poet (Italy)
46. Erling Kittelsen, Poet (Norway)
47. Tânia Tomé, Singer, Composer, Poet and Economist (Mozambique)
48. Rashid Boudjedra, Poet, novelist, playwright and critic (Algeria)
49. Ersi Sotiropoulos, Poet and novelist (Greece)
50. Mohammad Azizi, Poet and journalist (Afghanistan)
51. Emad Fouad, Poet and journalist (Egypt/ Belgium)
52. Dr.Arif Ali Albayrak, Poet, Cartoonist, Painter and Music Composer (Cyprus/Turkey)
53. Arturo Vázquez Sánchez, Poet (México)
54. José Manuel Solá Gómez, Poet, Writer (Puerto Rico)
55. Annabel Villar, Poet (Uruguay/Spain)
56. Stephanos Stephanides, Poet, professor of literature (Cyprus)
57. Peter Völker, Poet (Germany)
58. José Francisco Mejía Ramírez, Poet and Writer (Honduras)
59. Reza Heyrani, Poet (Iran)
60. Hadi Hazara, Poet (Afghanistan)

61. Nelly Elías de Benavente, Poet, Delegada de IALAYA – Instituto del libro Argentino y Americano (Argentina)

62. Rahela Yar, Poet (Afghanistan)

63. Werewere-Liking Gnepo, Poet and playwright and performer (Ivory Coast)

64. Marjorie Evasco, Poet and Teacher of Literature (Philippines)

65. Robert Max Steenkist, Poet, photographer and entrepeneur (Netherland/ Colombia)

66. Joseph Mwantuali, Poet (Clinton, New York, USA)

67. François Szabo, Poet (France)

68. Gaston Bellemare D.h.c., C.M., O.Q. Président Festival International de la Poésie/ Fédération des festivals internationaux de poésie (Québec, Canada)

69. Santiago B. Villafania, Poet (Philippines)

70. Jacobo Rauskin, Poet (Asunción, Paraguay)

71. Gertrude Fester, Poet and writer (South Africa)

72. Howard Fergus, Poet (Montserrat West Indies)

73. Prof.Dr.Sc. Ivan Djeparoski, Poet and philosopher (Skopje, R. Macedonia)

74. Nancy Huston, Novelist and essayist (Canada)

75. Elfriede Jelinek, Writer (Austria)

76. Tozan Alkan, Poet and translator (Istanbul/Turkey)

77. Euphrase Kezilahabi, Poet and novelist (Tanzania)

78. Fernando Sabido Sánchez, Poet (Spain)

79. Elyas Alavi, Poet (Afghanistan)

80. Parwiz Kawa, Poet (Afghanistan)

81. Dr.Homaira Nakhat Dastgirzada, Poet (Afghanistan)

82. Dawood Hakimi, Poet (Afghanistan)

83. Julieta Valero, Poet (Spain)

84. Hatto Fischer, Philosopher, Poet und Co-ordinator of Poiein kai Prattein (Germany)

85. Winston Morales Chavarro, Poet (Colombia)

86. Al Hunter, Poet(Anishinaabe Nation, Canada)

87. Siki Dlanga, Writer and poet (South Africa)

88. Carey Lenehan, Poet and Writer for Peace (London, UK)

89. Ernesto Carrión Poeta (Ecuador)

90. Rira Abbasi, Poet, writer and director of International peace poetry festival (Iran)

91. Mindy Zhang, Poet and translator (China-USA)

92. Haroon Rahoon, Poet (Afghanistan)

93. Samay Hamed, Poet (Afghanistan)

94. S.Asrar Hamed Muqtader "Vesta",Poet and Reporter (Afghanestan, presently Refugee in Turkey)

95. Raihan Yousef ,Poet and Reporter (Afghanestan, presently Refugee in Turkey)

96. Akwasi Aidoo, Poet (USA)

97. Robin Ngangom, Poet, translator, teacher (India)

98. Rafael Patiño Góez, Poet and translator (Colombia)

99. Sonja Harter, Poet (Vienna, Austria)

100. Parvaneh Torkamani, Poet and Social Worker (United States of America)

101. Fathieh Saudi, Poet (Jordan/UK)

102. Bengt Bertg, Poet and publisher (Sweden)

103. Sigurdur Pálsson, poet, (Iceland)

104. Tamer Öncül, Poet (Nicosia/Cyprus)

105. Partaw Naderi, Poet (Afghanistan)

106. Zeki Ali, Poet (Cyprus)

107. Leopoldo Castilla, Poeta (Argentina)

108. Rachel Tzvia Back, Poet (Israel)

109. Michael Augustin, Poet & Festival Director (Germany)

110. Mildred K Barya, Poet (Uganda)

111. Nicole Cage, Poet (Martinique)

112. Hafizullah Shariati, Poet (Afghanistan)

113. Abotalib Mozaffari, Poet (Afghanistan)

114. Saburullah Siasang, Poet (Afghanistan)

115. Nawzar Ilyas, Poet (Afghanistan)

116. Sam Hamill, Poet (USA)

117. Galvarino Orellana, Poet, writer and Secretary General of "Frente Cultural Bolivariano Internacional" (Chile)

118. Regina Dyck, Festival Director (Bremen, Germany)

119. David Huerta, Poet (Mexico)

120. Veronica Murguia, novelist (Mexico)

121. Gahston Saint-Fleur, Poet, Writter and Executive Director of Foundation PROCULTURA/PROKILTI (Haiti)

122. Miguel Aníbal Perdomo, Poet (Dominican Republic)

123. Amiri Baraka, Poet (USA)

124. Amina Baraka, Poet (USA)

125. Charl-Pierre Naude, Poet (South Africa)

126. Dunya Mikhail, Poet (Iraq)

127. Bei Dao, Poet (China)

128. Agus R. Sarjono, Poet & Editor in Chief Journal of

Criticism (Indonesia)

129. Nuno Júdice, Poet (Portugal)

130. Birgitta Jonsdottir, Poetician, Member of the Icelandic Parliament for the Movement & chairperson of the International Modern Media Institution (Iceland)

131. Reza Baraheni, Novelist, poet, critic, and political activist (Iran)

132. Peter Curman, Poet (Sweden)

133. Lyerka Bonanno, Poeta (Venezuela)

134. Grace R. Monte de Ramos, Poet (Philippines)

135. Geoffrey Philp, Poet, novelist, and playwright (Jamaica, West Indies)

136. BINYOU-BI-HOMB Marius Yannick, Poet (Cameroon)

137. Noria Adel, Poet, writer and visual artist (Algiers, Algeria)

138. Shakor Nazari, Poet, Editor, Head of Afghanistan Literature House In Kabul and Member of Afghanistan Independent Human Rights Commission (AIHRC) (Afghanistan)

139. Tsead Bruinja, Poet (Amsterdam, The Netherlands)

140. Bernard Noël, Poet (France)

141. Lic. Gerardo Paz Delgado, Poet, Secretario Nacional por Uruguay del Movimiento Internacional Poetas del Mundo. (Uruguay)

142. Christian Salmon, essayist and ex director of the International Parliament of Writers, (France)

143. Mark Lipman, Poet (USA)

144. Chirag Bangdel, Poet, artist and writer (Nepal)

145. Zolani Mkiva, Poet (South Africa)

146. Elena Armenescu, Poet (Romania)

147. D.M. Reyes, Poet and Literature Teacher (Philippines)

148. Tom Egeland, Author and critic (Norway)

149. Hildebrando Pérez Grande, Poet, Premio de Poesía Casa de las Américas (Peru)

150. Rodolfo Dada, Poet (Costa Rica)

151. Jean Portante, Novelist, poet, translator, journalist (Luxembourg/France)

152. Gonzalo Márquez Cristo, Poeta (Colombia)

153. Antonio Correa Losada, Poeta (Colombia)

154. Amparo Osorio, Poeta (Colombia)

155. Héctor Rosales, Poet (Uruguay/España)

156. Anthony L. Tan, Poet, fictionist, essayist, and teacher of literature (Philippines)

157. Myriam Montoya, Poet (Colombia/ France)

158. Jim Byron, musician (USA)

159. Carlos Piera, Writer (Spain)

160. Camila Charry Noriega, Poet (Colombia)

161. Harold Trujillo Torres, Caricaturista de opinión periódico El Espectador (Colombia)

162. Lucia Ortiz Corredor, Poet (Colombia)

163. Julio César Goyes Narváez, Poet (Colombia)

164. Julio César Goyes Narváez, Poet/ IECO-Instituto de Estudios en Comunicación y Cultura/ Universidad Nacional de Colombia (Colombia)

165. Alonso Sáenz M., Promotor de Lectura (Colombia)

166. Carmen Calatayud, Poet and nonfiction writer (USA)

167. Eduardo Emilio Esparza, Artista Plastico (Colombia)
168. Canéla A. Jaramillo, Poet, Author, Editor (United States)
169. Claribel Alegría, Poet, essayist, novelist, and journalist (Nicaragua)
170. Jill Schoolman, Publisher (USA)
171. Marco Antonio Campos, Poet (Mexico)
172. Marion Bethel, Poet (Bahamas)
173. Eleonora Parachini, Artista, (Colombia)
174. Juan Carlos Mestre, Poet and writer (Spain)
175. Ostap Nožak, writer and translator (Ukraine)
176. Stephane Chaumet, Poet (France)
177. Lic. Gerardo Paz Delgado, Poet, Secretario Nacional por Uruguay del Movimiento Internacional Poetas del Mundo. (Uruguay)
178. Julian Hector Gutierrez, Poet and writer (Colombia)
179. Francisco Sánchez Jiménez, Writer (Colombia)
180. Fredy Yezzed, Writer (Colombia/ Argentina)
181. Eusebio Sánchez Clavijo, Writer (Colombia)
182. Jose Yezid Morales, Poet and Painter (Colombia)
183. Helena Iriarte, Novelista y profesora universitaria de literatura (Colombia)
184. Paul Disnrad, Poet (Colombia/ Serbia)
185. Paul Dutton, Poet, Fiction Writer, Essayist and Musician (Canada)
186. Coral Bracho, Poeta (México)
187. Fanny Moreno Ospina, poeta (colombiana)
188. Martha Ennix, Artista plástica (colombiana)

189. Víctor López Rache Poeta y ensayista (Colombia)

190. María LeMarie, Writer and painter (Colombia)

191. Bassem Al Meraiby, Poet (Iraq- Sweden)

192. Manuel Pachón, Poeta y Maestro (Colombiano)

193. Maruja Vieira, Poet and journalist (Colombia)

194. Juan Carlos Acevedo Ramos, Poet (Colombia)

195. Roberta J. Hill, poet and writer, (Oneida) (Madison, Wisconsin in the U. S.)

196. Dieudonné Ewomsan, Poet (Togo)

197. Carlos Fajardo Fajardo, Poet (Colombia)

198. Qassim Haddad, Poet (Bahrain)

199. Neeli Cherkovski, Poet (USA)

200. Fabio Martinez, Escritor (Colombia)

201. Morela Maneiro, Poet (Venezuela)

202. Sayed Hegab, Poet (Egypt)

203. Zoran Anchevski, poet, translator, professor of literature (Macedonia)

204. Liv Lundberg, Poet, Writer, Professor (Norway)

205. Pia Tafdrup, Poet and Writer (Denmark)

206. Micere Githae Mugo , Poet, Playwright, Scholar and Activist (Kenya)

207. Angye Gaona, Poeta (Colombia)

208. Allison Hedge Coke, Poet and writer (US)

209. Matthew Shenoda, Poet (USA/Egypt)

210. Chiqui Vicioso, Poet (Dominican Republic)

211. Aref Pejman, Poet, Author, and Associate Professor (Afghanistan)

212. Fredy Chikangana, Poeta y Escritor Quechua Yanakuna Mitmak (Colombia)
213. Ramiz Rovshan, Poet and writer (Azerbaijan)
214. Liam Ó Muirthile, Poet (Ireland)
215. Nguyen Quang Thieu, Poet (Vietnam)
216. Andrei Khadanovich, Poet (Belarus)
217. Alberto Nessi, poeta e scrittore (Switzerland)
218. Hermes Vargas. Poeta (Spain)
219. Chris Abani, Poet and writer (Nigeria/USA)
220. Abdourahman WABERI, Poet (Djibouti)
221. Beppe Costa, poet, novelist and publisher (Italy)
222. Stefania Battistella, Poet (Italy)
223. Senem Gökel, Poet, researcher, instructor (Cyprus)
224. Ingrid Wickström, Poet and translater (Sweden)
225. Priya Sarukkai Chabria, Poet, writer and translator (India)
226. Homero Aridjis, Poet and novelist, President Emeritus of PEN International (Mexico)
227. Gemino H. Abad, Poet, professor emeritus of literature and creative writing (Philippines)
228. Vasyl Makhno, Poet (Ukraine/USA)
229. Vincent O'Sullivan, Poet (New Zealand)
230. Joy Harjo, Poet and musician (Mvskoke Nation, USA)
231. Gioconda Belli, Poet and novelist (Nicaragua)
232. Francisco de Asís Fernández, Poet and President of the International Poetry Festival, Nicaragua (Nicaragua)
233. Gloria Gabuardi, Poet (Nicaragua)
234. Alexandra Büchler, Director of Literature Across Frontiers

(Czech Republic/UK)

235. Nora Atalla, poète, romancière et nouvelliste (Québec, Canada)

236. Moya Cannon, Poet (Irland)

237. Michèle Blanchet, poète de Québec (Canada)

238. Nyein Way, Poet, Performance artist and educator (Myanmar)

239. Max.N.RIPPON poet (Marie-Galante, Guadeloupe)

240. Omar Pérez, Poet, writer and translator (Cuba)

241. Jared Angira, Poet (Kenya)

242. Rashidah Ismaili, Poet (Benin)

243. Raquel Chalfi, Poet and writer (Israel)

244. Blanca Andreu, Poet (Spain)

245. Michaël Glück, Poet (France)

246. Stefaan van den Bremt, Poet and Honorary chairman of PEN FLANDERS (Flanders, Belgium)

247. Jan Owen, Writer (Australia)

248. Vyacheslav Kupriyanov, Poet (Russia)

249. Geneviève Morin, Poet (Québec, Canada)

250. Yiorgos Chouliaras, Poet (Greece)

251. Quito Nicolaas, Writer/Poet (The Netherlands)

252. Simón Zavala Guzmán, Poeta y ensayista (Ecuador)

253. Timo Berger, Poet and publisher (Germany)

254. Ceaití Ní Bheildiúin, Poet (Ireland)

255. Jean Clarence Lambert, Poet, translator, essayist and art critic (France)

256. Antonio Preciado, Poet (Ecuador)

257. Manal Al-Sheikh, Poet and writer (Iraq/ Norway)

258. Yasin Khamosh, Poet and journalist (Afghanistan)

259. Valeriu Stancu, Poet, novelist and translator (Romania)

260. Aju Mukhopadhyay, Poet, essayist, feature and fiction writer (India)

261. GILMA DE LOS RÍOS TOBÓN, Poeta y periodista (Colombia)

262. Breyten Breytenbach, Poet (South Africa / France)

263. John Hegley, Poet (England)

264. Latif Nazemi, Poet (Afghanistan)

265. Carolina Escobar Sarti, Poet (Guatemala)

266. Raphael Urweider, Poet and President of the Swiss writers association (AdS)

267. Andrei Khadanovich, Poet (Belarus)

268. Igor Ursenco, Escritor, Ensayista, Traductor Freelance (Republica de Moldavia / Rumania)

269. Henry Braun, Poet (Weld, Maine, USA)

270. Edvino Ugolini, Poet and activist for human rights net of artists against war and President of associazione interculturale penombre (Trieste, Italy)

271. Mairym Cruz-Bernal, Poet (Puerto Rico)

272. Len Anderson, Poet (Santa Cruz, California, USA)

273. Rassool Jibraeel Snyman, Poet (South Africa)

274. Madeline Millán, poet (Puerto Rico/New York City)

275. Hilde Susan Jaegtnes, poet and screenwriter (Norway)

276. Ngwatilo Mawiyoo, Poet & Performing Artist (Kenya)

277. David Howard, Poet (Aotearoa/New Zealand)

278. Juan Cameron, Poet (Chile)

279. Salim REGAMI, Poet (Algeria)

280. Maya Trace Borhani, Poet & Educator (USA/Canada)

281. Iryna Vikyrchak, poet, director of the International Poetry Festival Meridian (Czernowitz, Ukraine)

282. Séamas Cain, Poet and playwright (Northern Ireland/ USA)

283. Jan Erik Vold, Poet , writer, translator (Norway)

284. Qanbarali Tabesh, Poet (Afghanistan)

285. Shirin Aitmatova, Poet and Member of Kyrgyz Parliament (Kyrgyzstan)

286. Roza Aitmatova, Journalist, writer and political analyzer (Kyrgyzstan)

287. Cholpon Jakupova, Wrtiter and women defender (Kyrgyzstan)

288. Djumanaliev Tuncholot Dadyevich, writer, dean of " National University Of Kyrgyzstan" Philosophy Professor (Kyrgyzstan)

289. Selbi Jumayeva, Writer, Poet and Women rights defender (Kyrgyzstan)

290. Marat Usmanov, Poet, Philosophy Professor at AUCA (Kyrgyzstan)

291. Adamkulova Chinara, "Dean of Kyrgyz-European faculty of Kyrgyz National University" Women Rights defender and Poet (Kyrgyzstan)

292. Andrew Wachtel, Poet, Writer, Dean of AUCA in Kyrgyzstan (Kyrgyzstan)

293. Isabel Gómez, Poeta (Chile)

294. Magda Carneci, Poet and president of the Romanian PEN (poet, Romania)
295. Áine Moynihan, poet and actor (Ireland)
296. Thomas Harris, Writer (USA)
297. Luisa Vicioso Sánchez, Poet and women and children rights activist (Dominican Republic)
298. Muhsin Al-Ramli, Poet and writer (Iraq)
299. Heiko Strunk, Poet and poetry website co-ordinator (Germany)
300. Carmen Berenguer, Poet (Chile)
301. Enrique Hernández-D'Jesús, Poeta y fotógrafo (Venezuela)
302. Vicente Rodríguez Nietzsche, Poet (Puerto Rico)
303. Ban'ya Natsuishi, Haiku poet (Japan)
304. Joe Richey, Poet (USA)
305. Teresa Colom, Poet (Andorra)
306. Christina Pacosz, Poet (USA)
307. Francesca Randazzo, Poet and Sociologist (Honduras/Spain)
308. Sainkho Namtchylak, Singer and poet (Siberia/ Austria)
309. Menna Elfyn, Poet, playwright and Director of Creative Writing University of Wales Trinity Saint David (Wales/ United Kingdom)
310. Jack Mapanje, Poet and linguist (Malawi/UK)
311. Mohammad Vaezi, Poet and journalist (Afghanistan)
312. Jessie Kleemann, Poet, performance artist, writer, cultural consultant (Greenland/Denmark)
313. Sunita Zade, Poet and journalist (India)
314. Khalid Albudoor, Poet (United Arab Emirates)

315. Sadegh Dehghan, Poet (Afghanistan)

316. Reza Talebi, Poet (Azerbaijan/ Turkey)

317. James O'Hara, Poet (USA)

318. Sayed Zia Qasemi, Poet (Afghanistan)

319. Braňo Hochel, Poet, Editor-in-Chief of RAK (Slovakia)

320. Eugenia Sánchez Nieto, Poeta (Colombia)

321. Mary Smith, Poet, writer, and journalist (Scotland)

322. Ernesto P. Santiago, Poet and writer (Philippines)

323. Jorge Boccanera, Poeta (Argentino)

324. Farzana Marie, Poet (USA)

325. David Meltzer, Poet and musician (USA)

326. Raks Morakabe Seakhoa, Poet and activist (South Africa)

327. Jaime García Pulido, Poet and writer (Colombia)

328. Mahnaz Badihian, Poet (Iran/ USA)

329. John Curl, Poet (San Francisco, United States)

330. William Pérez Vega, Poet (Puerto Rico)

331. Gemino H. Abad, Poet (Philippines)

332. Phillippa Yaa De Villiers, Poet (South Africa)

333. Simón Zavala Guzmán, Poet and journalist (Ecuador)

334. Ali Abdollahi, Poet and translator (Iran)

335. Juan Diego Velásquez, Poet (Colombia)

336. Yolanda Pantin, Poet (Venezuela)

337. Erkut Tokman, Poet, actor, visual artist and translator (Turkey)

Unpublished poets:

338. Mir Hussain Mahdavi, Exiled freelance writer and poet (Afghanistan)

339. Basi Gol Sharifi, Poet (Afghanistan)
340. Leila Malekmohammadi, Poet and journalist (Iran/ Norway)
341. Sultan Haidari, Journalist and poet (Afghanistan)
342. Ali Hazara, Poet and movie maker (Afghanistan)
343. Hossein Pooya, Poet (Afghanistan)
344. Sakhi dad Hatef, Poet (Afghanistan)
345. Maryam Turkmani, Poet (Afghanistan)
346. Razi Mohebi, Poet and movie maker (Afghanistan)
347. Fereshta Ziai, Poet, pedagog and youth mentor (Afghanistan/Sweden)
348. Laila Haidari, Poet and director of Life is Beautiful Organization (Afghanistan)
349. Zalmay Kave, Poet (Afghanistan)
350. Ruhullah Vaezi, Poet (Afghanistan)
351. Ali Jafari, Poet (Afghanistan)
352. Rayhana Akhondzada, Poet (Afghanistan)
353. Zakia Askarzadah, Poet (Afghanistan)

SUPPORTERS

1. Jette Ní Mhaolcatha, Translator and anthropologist (Denmark)
2. Robert Maier, M.A., Producer, Author, Professor of Broadcasting, Gaston College (USA)
3. Basir Ahang, Journalist and human rights activist (Afghanistan, Italy)
4. Akbar Khurasani, Painter (Ukraine, Afghanistan)

5. Bashir Bakhtiari, Journalist, cartoonist and documentary maker (Afghanistan, Australia)
6. Akbar Danesh, Radio Paywand Owner and director (Bamiyan, Afghanistan)
7. Dr. Yar Sana, Publisher of Andisha-e-Nau monthly magazine (Afghanistan/ Canada)
8. Abdullah Khodada, Social activist and president of Afghanistan Reformists
9. Sultan Haidari, Director of Bokhdi News Agency (Afghanistan)
10. Dr. S. Ashrafzai, Economist" and writer (Afghanistan)
11. Mona Bentzen, Visual artist, video art curator and documentary filmmaker (Norway)
12. Mohammd Ishaq Fayyaz, Writer and journalist (Afghanistan/ Turkey)
13. Khaliq Ebrahimi, Interpreter (Afghanistan)
14. Jawad Hamdard Kia, Photographer and freelance journalist (Afghansitan)
15. Hassina Burgan, Actress. visual artist (United Kingdom)
16. Laura Bursh, Writer, musician and artist (USA)
17. Xuebin Burican, Journalist and artist (Romania)
18. John Burgan, Senior Lecturer and Documentary Filmmaker (United Kingdom)
19. Wais Orozgani, Director of Sobhi Nawin Association (Mazar i Sharif, Afghanistan)
20. Besmellah Rezaee, lawyer/solicitor and freelance writer (Australia/ Afghanistan)
21. Jan Evans, community advocate (Brisbanc Australia)

22. Mary Estcourt, Community Advocate (Hobart, Australia)
23. Kjell H. Maere, Writer (Norway)
24. Evy Ellingvag, Human rights activist and writer (Norway)
25. Beret Werner, Activist (Norway)
26. Anna Da Silva Santos, Activist (Australia)
27. Muhammad Ali Sultani, Professor at Polytechnical University of Kabul (Afghanistan)
28. Frederika Steen, Human rights activist and former immigration officer (Australia)
29. Harold Trujillo Torres, Cartoonist (Colombia)
30. Rosemary Stanfield-Johnson, PhD, Associate Professor, Department of History, University of Minnesota Duluth (USA)
31. Mohammad Mostafaei, Lawyer (Iran/ Norway)
32. Hussain Zahedi, Journalist and activist (Afghanistan/Canada)
33. Nicole Valentini, Activist (Italy)
34. Davood Mousavi, Photographer and blogger (Iran/ Sweden)
35. Kawa Gharj, Activist and blogger (Afghanistan)
36. M. Kazim wahidi, Activist and blogger (Afghanistan)
37. Rahmatullah Alizadah, Journalist (Afghanistan)
38. Mortaza Rahimi, Journalist (Afghanistan)
39. Lou Dingle, Activist (Australia)
40. Ali Payam, Writer (Afghanistan)

Translators

All poets have translated their own poems except the following:

- Luis Rafael Gálvez
- Walter G. Andrews
- David Mason
- Yiorgos Chouliaras
- Lucy James
- Patricia Lidia
- Javier Zamudio
- Jane Kostas
- Andrew Evans
- Erín Moure
- Mony Zinati
- Daniel Borzutzky
- Nicole Valentini
- Vivian Eden
- Graham and Peggy W. Reid

Photo Credits

All photos are copyrighted by the poets except the following:

- David Belcher
- Nelson Garrido
- Tone Gellein
- James and Oscar
- Borzelli Photography
- www.fabricainutil.com
- Hanna Quevedo Photography
- Photo of James and Oscar
- www.corinamoscovich.blogspot.com
- Wikipedia
- www.festivaldepoesiademedellin.org
- www.alusainc.wordpress.com
- www.letras.s5.com

Hazara Rights

www.HazaraRights.com
Poets and Writers Worldwide
Against Hazara Genocide

Hazara People
International Network
www.HazaraPeople.com

www.ingramcontent.com/pod-product-compliance
Lightning Source LLC
Chambersburg PA
CBHW020631300426
44112CB00007B/77